Level 1 Certificate for IT Users
for City & Guilds

# Using E-mail

Level
1

## for Office XP

Tina Lawton

**Endorsed by**
**City&**
**Guilds**

**www.heinemann.co.uk**
✓ Free online support
✓ Useful weblinks
✓ 24 hour online ordering

**01865 888058**

**Heinemann**
*Inspiring generations*

Heinemann Educational Publishers
Halley Court, Jordan Hill, Oxford, OX2 8EJ
A division of Harcourt Education Ltd

OXFORD MELBOURNE AUCKLAND
JOHANNESBURG BLANTYRE GABORONE
IBADAN PORTSMOUTH NH(USA) CHICAGO

First published in 2004
2007  2006  2005  2004
10  9  8  7  6  5  4  3  2  1

A catalogue record for this book is available from the British Library on request.

ISBN 0 435 46276 8

Typeset by Techset Ltd, Gateshead
Printed and bound in Great Britain by Thomson Litho Ltd, Glasgow

Tel: 01865 888058  www.heinemann.co.uk

## Acknowledgements
The authors and publishers would like to thank the following for permission to reproduce screenshots: Microsoft (throughout book); Figure 1.4 Virgin Net; page 5 AOL; Figure 1.5 Freeserve; Figure 1.6 Freeserve, Tiscali, Virgin Net; Figure 1.7 Freeserve; Figure 3.2 BlackStar; Figure 3.4 Virgin Net; Figures 3.20–3.21 Adobe Reader®; Figures 4.6–4.7 GlobalSCAPE.

The publishers have made every effort to trace the copyright holders, but if they have inadvertently overlooked any, they will be pleased to make the necessary arrangements at the first opportunity.

## Websites
Please note that the examples of websites suggested in this book were up to date at the time of writing. It is essential for tutors to preview each site before using it to ensure that the URL is still accurate and the content is appropriate. We suggest that tutors bookmark useful sites and consider enabling students to access them through the school or college intranet.

## Limit of liability/disclaimer of warranty
The accuracy and completeness of the information provided herein are not guaranteed or warranted to produce any particular results, and the advice and strategies contained herein may not be suitable for every individual.

# Contents

# Introduction

City & Guilds e-Quals is an exciting new range of IT qualifications developed with leading industry experts. These comprehensive, progressive awards cover everything from getting to grips with basic IT to gaining the latest professional skills.

The range consists of both user and practitioner qualifications. User qualifications (Levels 1–3) are ideal for those who use IT as part of their job or in life generally, while Practitioner qualifications (Levels 2–3) have been developed for those who need to boost their professional skills in, for example, networking or software development.

e-Quals boasts on-line testing and a dedicated web site with news and support materials and web-based training. The qualifications reflect industry standards and meet the requirements of the National Qualifications Framework.

With e-Quals you will not only develop your expertise, you will gain a qualification that is recognised by employers all over the world.

This unit is about using e-mail – a fast, effective way of sending and receiving messages from anywhere in the world. In this electronic age, using the Internet to communicate has proved to be very popular indeed, with many millions of e-mail messages crossing the globe daily. E-mails help speed business along as well as keeping you in touch with relatives and friends in far-flung places (or perhaps nearer to home!)

Using e-mail you can send not just text messages, but files, images, programs, even music, right to someone's desktop. Critics suggest that the art of writing is dead, but the traffic of e-mail messages through any ISP's server must surely prove that it isn't true! Working through the sections, you will be able to learn about a wide range of topics from attachments to aliases, contacts to connecting, and sending to signatures. You will be able to find out how to keep in touch and keep your computer safe.

Throughout the unit there are challenges to test your knowledge and opportunities to practise your skills. At the end of the book there are assignments for you to use as practice to make sure you're absolutely ready to pass the real thing.

Although this book covers the syllabus for the City & Guilds IT Users Level 1 Certificate Unit 007, it would be just as helpful for anyone wanting to learn how to use e-mail.

## Acknowledgements

My grateful thanks to: Stuart for his constant support and understanding – not to mention the endless cups of tea; Keith and Anna for introducing me to the joys of e-mail; all my friends and colleagues who unknowingly feature in the message lists, especially Lesley who sent me an attachment when I needed it most!; last, but not least, Pen, for believing I could do it.

# Getting started

## You will learn to

- Describe in simple terms the hardware and software required to make appropriate use of services available via e-mail
- Describe what factors determine efficiency when sending and receiving e-mail messages
- Identify different ISP providers
- Describe e-mail as an electronic mail box and identify the elements of an e-mail address
- Describe how computers use protocols to move e-mails around
- Set up an e-mail program
  - ☐ Choose and obtain an e-mail address
  - ☐ Dial up a connection
  - ☐ Access an e-mail program
  - ☐ Shut down an e-mail program
- Use web-based e-mail
- Describe the advantages and disadvantages of using e-mail

## Introduction: A global network

### Information

To send and receive e-mails you need to have a computer and a link to the Internet.

When two computers are linked together to share information and resources, they form a network. Computer networks can be found in many organisations – in fact you may be part of a network when you log on to your computer at work or college. A computer which is not connected to a network is called a standalone machine, but you can't exchange data and files with other computers unless you transfer them to floppy disks first, which can be very time-consuming. Using a network makes it much easier to pass information to other computer users who are also linked into the network.

The Internet is a global network which links millions of computers and smaller networks in many countries across the world. Using the Internet, it is as easy to communicate with someone in Australia as it is to send a message to your work colleague at the next workstation. When you join this huge network, using your telephone line or cable connection, you can access the wealth of information and services provided on the Internet as well as being able to send and receive messages and files using e-mail.

**Figure 1.1** The Internet enables people throughout the world to communicate with one another by computer

## Equipment for connecting to the Internet

Getting connected requires certain hardware and software. First you'll need a **computer**, but it doesn't need to have the latest and fastest processor to be able to access the vast amounts of information on the Net or to send your e-mails around the world.

For a home computer you will need a **modem** to connect to your phone line. Your PC processes **digital** data, represented as either a 0 or a 1 (binary), by turning on or off a series of switches. Your telephone system is an **analogue** device which transmits signals in a continuous wave. A **modem** is a device which translates analogue signals into digital data and vice versa, and is called this because it **mo**dulates and **dem**odulates the signal so the telephone system and the computer can understand each other.

Modems can be external or internal, but in either case they need to be connected to both your telephone line and your computer. You will need to be able to access the Internet one way or another to send and receive e-mails. The most common way to do this is to register with an **ISP (Internet Service Provider)** who will act as your 'gateway' to the Internet as well as your e-mail post office.

### Information

To connect to the Internet using the newer technologies, such as Broadband, which transfers data at a much faster speed than the traditional phone lines, you will still need a modem, but it will be one that can cope with the high speed of data transfer. For broadband connections, modern technologies allow the modem to be connected to your computer via wireless signals, so you won't have cables to connect, thus making for a tidier workplace.

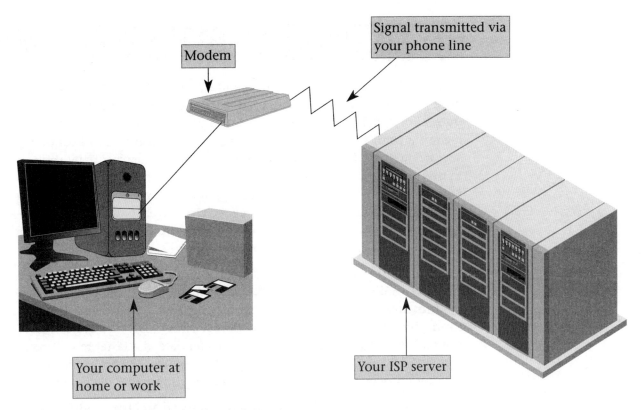

**Figure 1.2** How your computer is connected to the Internet

The final piece of the jigsaw is the **software** you need to connect to your ISP. This is called a **browser**, and is a program that translates the information on the Net into documents you can see on screen. Most browsers have other useful functions too, like access to e-mail, downloading files, saving web pages and allowing you to print out information. The browsers most people are familiar with are **Internet Explorer** and **Netscape**.

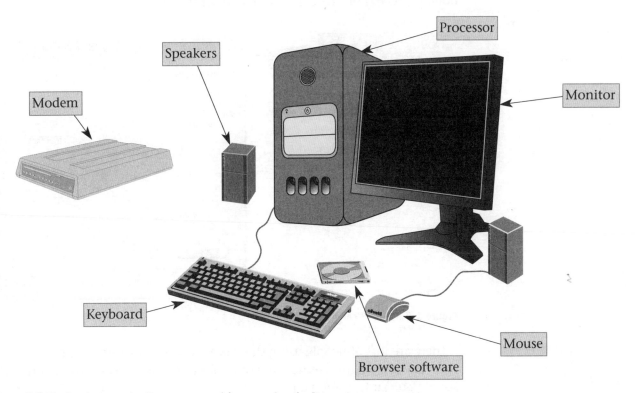

**Figure 1.3** The hardware and software you need for accessing the Internet

# How fast can you go?

As you will have gathered, one of the most essential bits of hardware you need to connect to the Internet is the modem. As the modem handles the transfer of data between the Internet and your computer, the speed at which it can transmit that data is critical. This speed is measured in **bits per second** (a bit is the smallest unit of memory or storage), usually shortened to **bps**. Most new computers these days will have modems with a speed of **56Kbps** (Kilobits per second). Anything much slower than this, and you may find yourself waiting a long time for web pages to download onto your screen or for your e-mail, complete with large file attachments, to land in your Inbox, which can be frustrating.

Any connection to the Internet using your normal phone line will be limited to 56Kbps. The speed of data transmission will also be decided by the **bandwidth** of the communication lines being used to make the connection. Some of the newer technologies like ISDN (Integrated Services Digital Network) and Broadband can transfer data at a faster rate. Broadband connections can download data at speeds of up to 512 Kbps, and, as technology develops, download speeds are getting faster all the time.

There is another factor, apart from modem speed and bandwidth, that can affect the rate of data transfer. Just like the main roads at rush hour, the Internet, which is often referred to as the Information Superhighway, can become a crawl as thousands of users log on at peak times. It's always worth checking the time if things seem to be very slow – it may just be because the businesses in America have suddenly connected to the Net at the start of their working day! Your modem software will usually tell you the speed of your connection when you are online. You can access this dialogue box by double clicking on the connected icon on the taskbar.

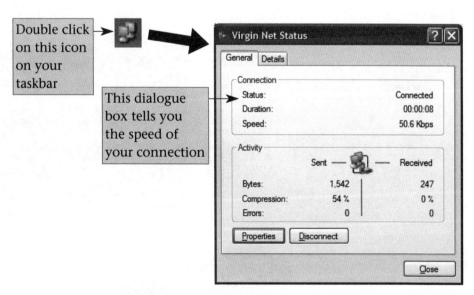

**Figure 1.4** Speed of connection

If there are lots of people using the server you are connected to, or if everyone is trying to connect to your ISP, then this too can slow down the speed you can transfer data.

Not surprisingly, if you're downloading big files or lots of graphics as attachments to your e-mails, it can seem to take forever. Your modem might be working at peak efficiency, but you need to remember that the bigger the file/graphic, the longer it will take to download.

## Online Services and Internet Service Providers

When you're thinking about getting connected to the Internet and being able to use the electronic mail service, the first decision you have to make is whether to go for an **Online Service** or an **Internet Service Provider (ISP)**.

### Online Service

There is really only one major contender in the Online Services – **AOL (America Online)**. It is very easy to obtain the software to sign up to this service; it is given as a free disc on the cover of most computer magazines and sometimes it will find its way through your letter box. Having got the CD-ROM with the software, signing up couldn't be easier. Load the software, which is really only a case of following the onscreen instructions (after you've put the CD in the CD drive, of course!), enter your debit or credit card number and then you're ready to go.

It is important not to confuse an Online Service with the Internet itself. When you've subscribed, you'll have joined a private club. There will be a whole range of members-only areas such as discussion forums, information and shopping facilities, as well as being able to access the Internet. An Online Service, such as AOL, tends to have good built-in help facilities, the members-only content should be safe for even small eyes to view, and it has an easy-to-use interface.

Online Services give you the Internet, e-mail and a bit more besides, but you have to pay for the privilege. An Online Service charges a fixed monthly fee, and then there's the cost of your phone calls on top, though the service might include subsidised call charges. You might also find that once outside the 'clubhouse' of the members-only area, your information doesn't travel quite as quickly as a direct connection to the Internet.

### Internet Service Providers

An Internet Service Provider does just that – provides the service to access the Internet. There are many ISPs available, and the choice can be bewildering for a newcomer to the Net. Essentially they are very similar, mainly using Internet Explorer or Netscape as their browser and Outlook Express or Netscape Mail as their e-mail program, but they will have different logos on the start-up screens, and may have different icons on your desktop.

An ISP runs a network that connects to other parts of the Internet. It has a bank of modems that you can call from your PC at home or work. The services your ISP provides don't just stop at Internet access, it can provide other important functions as well:

- Storing messages sent to you until you collect them next time you log on.
- Providing web space for you to upload your own information and web pages so that other people can access your site whether your computer is switched on or not.
- Providing other areas for subscribers to use, such as online magazines, chat rooms, information services.
- Multiple e-mail addresses, so that everyone in the family can have their own e-mail facilities.
- Providing help facilities if something goes wrong.

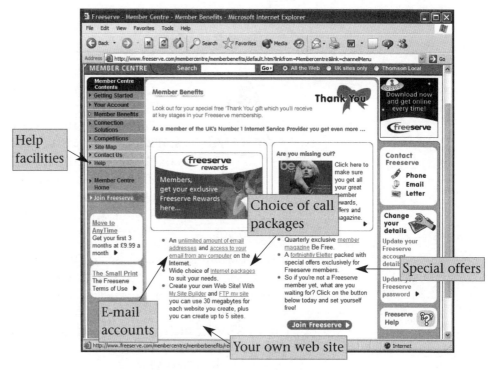

**Figure 1.5** The services an ISP can provide

Not all ISPs provide all these services, but many do. Your choice of ISP will depend on which of these services you might want.

As there are so many ISPs fighting for your custom, this is definitely good for you, the customer. Most of the ISPs now offer their services free, with no monthly subscription charge – you just pay for your phone calls. Some ISPs offer packages to make accessing the Internet cheaper, for example by giving free Internet calls during the evenings and weekends for a small monthly fee, or other similar premium rate services.

Most ISPs will provide the software you need which is already configured with all the complicated settings your computer needs to know to make the connection. It's usually only a case of putting the CD in the CD drive and following the onscreen instructions to install the software to get you up and running.

# What are the differences between ISPs?

**Figure 1.6** Logos of various ISPs

## Costs

Most ISPs offer free Internet access and you pay just for the cost of the phone calls. This can be as low as 1p per minute at weekends. It is also possible to pay a monthly fee of about £10 for free access at weekends and in the evenings, which could be better value.

One of the benefits of all this free access is that if you don't think the ISP you're using is giving a good service, you can simply change to another one and give them a try. Just a word of warning, however. Your e-mail account often comes with your ISP which provides you with the most important part of your address – the domain name – so changing ISPs might mean changing your e-mail address and letting everyone know. It's much the same process as when you move house, except that you can use special functions in your e-mail package to send this information to everyone in your address book.

The other benefit is that you can sign up to several ISPs and choose which one you use at any one time depending on the services and special offers that are available.

## Local connections

Most ISPs will have a **POP (Point of Presence)**; this is a point of access to the Net. The large providers will have many POPs all over the country, which means that you should only need to dial a local number to connect with your ISP. This is an important point because a local POP with a local phone number will mean only paying local phone call charges to access the Net.

If you can connect through a local number, you can talk to other computers anywhere in the world for just the cost of a local phone call. This means you can send e-mails, files, images, etc. to Australia much cheaper than using snail mail!

## Speeding

Using your normal telephone line your modem can connect to your ISP's modem at a maximum speed of 56Kbps (Kilobits per second). Most ISPs will support that speed of connection, but if you have something different, such as BT Home Highway or broadband, not all ISPs can support it.

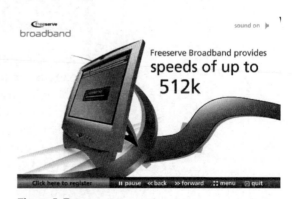

**Figure 1.7** Connection speed

## Setting up

It has already been mentioned that most ISPs will provide you with the software you need to load a browser, e-mail application and any other necessary software. As competition between the various ISPs is so strong, most providers will have software that is already pre-configured. It should just be a case of loading it and then dialling into your ISP to get your user name and password. Following the onscreen instructions should be straightforward, however most ISPs will provide a helpline if you get stuck. The only snag with this is that some ISPs charge a premium for their helpline service, anything up to £1 per minute, or more.

## E-mail

E-mail packages come as standard with the two most common browsers, Internet Explorer and Netscape. If your computer is used by several members of the family, it is always preferable to have separate e-mail addresses so that your messages stay private. Most providers will offer multiple e-mail addresses, but if you've got a big family, the five offered by many providers might not be enough.

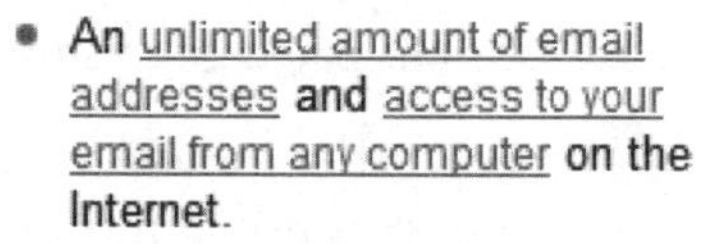

- An unlimited amount of email addresses and access to your email from any computer on the Internet.

**Figure 1.8** You can have access to more than one e-mail address

## Web space

Most ISPs will offer web space so that you can have your own web site. The amount of web space offered will vary from ISP to ISP.

## What else?

With so many providers offering free access, some will provide extra services such as news services, travel information and chat rooms. There may be special offers at any time, such as special deals for goods or services.

# Electronic mail

One of the quickest ways of communicating with others on a network is to use **electronic mail** or **e-mail** as it is usually called. This is a method of sending letters, memos, pictures and sounds from one computer to another. If you are at home, you may use a modem to connect to your phone line so that you can send e-mails to anywhere in the world and receive e-mails in reply. This is often quicker than 'snail mail' (the name sometimes used for the postal system) and, usually, just for the cost of a local phone call.

As you will have realised, to send and receive e-mails you will need some basic equipment: a computer, a modem, an e-mail program, such as Outlook Express, and an account with an Internet Service Provider to access the Internet. The e-mail system is very much like a postal service, an **electronic**

**mail box** in fact. You send e-mails through your ISP's post office, to the post offices of your recipients' ISPs, where the messages wait until they next log on.

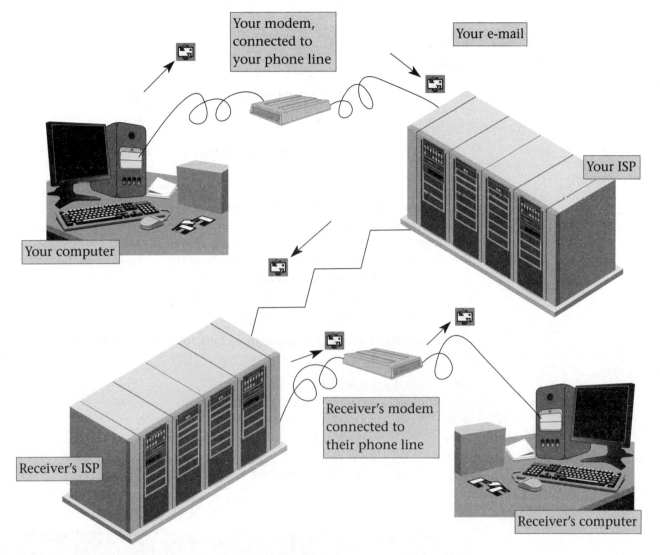

**Figure 1.9** The journey an e-mail makes from sender to receiver

If you are on a network, you will be able to send messages to other people in your organisation as well as sending them to people outside the network through a phone line or ISDN (Integrated Services Digital Network) connection or a broadband connection. Whether you are sending or receiving e-mails internally or externally you will need to have e-mail software, such as Microsoft **Outlook Express**, installed on your computer or network. There are many e-mail programs available, most of which perform similar tasks of sending and receiving e-mail messages, although they might look different and some may have more advanced features than others. Netscape Mail and Eudora are among some of the other popular e-mail programs. Most of the software provided by ISPs will have e-mail programs included.

## Finding the right address

With so many millions of computers forming the Internet, it is essential that each computer knows where it is and where all the other computers are. This is done by means of unique addresses, called **Internet Protocol**

**(IP)** addresses. IP addresses are usually in the form of a series of numbers which would be difficult to remember, so each computer is given a name too – this is the **domain name**. This is usually in three parts and gives details about where the computer is located.

To send an e-mail to someone, you will need to know his or her e-mail address. This is a unique address that will look something like the one shown below:

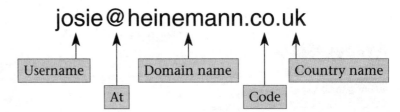

- **Username**  The name or nickname of the person.
- **Domain name**  The unique address of the computer. This has three main sections that tell you where the computer is.
  - □ **heinemann** – the organisation where the user works or the **Internet Service Provider's** name
  - □ **co** – this tells you the type of organisation
  - □ **uk** – this tells you the country.

There are several types of organisations and you can tell from the e-mail address which type it is:

| | |
|---|---|
| **ac** | an academic organisation |
| **co** or **com** | a commercial organisation |
| **edu** | an educational institution |
| **gov** | a government body |
| **net** | an organisation involved in running the Net |
| **org** | a non-profit-making organisation |

# Protocols

Internet e-mail uses two main protocols to move the messages around the global network. It uses **Simple Mail Transfer Protocol (SMTP)** to send messages and **Post Office Protocol (POP)** to receive messages. As these standards are universal, the software sending and receiving e-mails and the servers that handle the messages can talk to each other even with very different computer systems. Your e-mail program needs to know the names of the servers (your ISP's mainframe computers) that handle the mail. It may be something like: smtp.supersurfer.net and pop.supersurfer.net, although your ISP will be able to tell you, if their software isn't already pre-configured.

Networks which operate within a large company or organisation may use **Internet Message Access Protocol (IMAP)**.

The main body of an e-mail message is just plain text, but it used to be a rather hit and miss operation to send a file attached to it, as the programs weren't as capable as they are today. It is very much easier with modern e-mail applications to send all types of files as attachments, such as video clips, photos, large documents, etc.

The text system that allows ordinary numbers and letters, punctuation marks such as spaces and tabs, plus a few special characters, but no formatting or font information, is called **ASCII**. This is a format that can be recognised by almost any type of computer. When you send an e-mail with a file attachment, the program converts the data into ASCII for sending with the message and the recipient's e-mail program at the other end converts the data back again. This works well as long as the system used to convert the data is the same in both e-mail programs. There are three systems in use, although the **MIME** system is probably the one most commonly used:

- **Uuencode**   The original and rather crude conversion system which broke the ASCII text into chunks.
- **MIME (Multipurpose Internet Mail Extensions)**   The much more sophisticated successor to Uuencoding. This identifies the type of file being sent and automatically converts without any help at each end of the process.
- **BinHex**   This system is mostly used on Macintosh computers and is similar to Uuencode.

If your e-mail program and your recipient's e-mail program use different systems you would just end up with gobbledegook! However, most e-mail programs today will use MIME, and you should be able to send your files without any problems, although if your recipient complains that they only get gibberish, then perhaps this might be the reason.

## Setting up an e-mail account

To connect to the Internet and use e-mail, you will need a browser such as Internet Explorer or Netscape, and an e-mail program such as Outlook Express or Netscape Mail. If you are using Windows Operating System, Internet Explorer and Outlook Express will probably be installed on your computer. Both browsers and e-mail programs can be found on many computer magazine cover CD-ROMs, or one or the other will be provided by your ISP.

The **New Connection Wizard** makes setting up your Internet account a fairly straightforward business, although if you are using an ISP's set-up CD-ROM, most of this process will be done for you.

Your ISP will provide you with the information you need to complete the set-up process, including your ISP's telephone number (the one to access their servers, not their Helpline!).

You will have to decide on your user name and password, but choosing a password is a serious business. You will need to remember it, and you will certainly want to keep it secret, otherwise people may be able to log into your mailbox and read your personal e-mails.

You will also be able to choose your e-mail address, but you might need to have a second or third choice available if someone else has already chosen the one you want. If your name is John Smith, you can imagine that there are probably quite a few such John Smiths who have asked for j.smith as their e-mail name! It's a good idea to have a few other suggestions ready, just in case. Remember that your e-mail address will also have the '@domain name.co.uk', or similar, after your e-mail name.

With all this information to hand you can now follow the steps to get connected using the **New Connection Wizard**, and within minutes you can be sending (and receiving) your first e-mails!

| Task 1.1 | Making the connection |

If you are making a new connection to an ISP, the **New Connection Wizard** will guide you through the process of connecting to your ISP, but read the instructions on each screen carefully. This example shows the steps for setting up a connection to your ISP manually using a phone line and modem.

## Method

I   Using the **Start** menu, locate and select the **New Connection Wizard**.

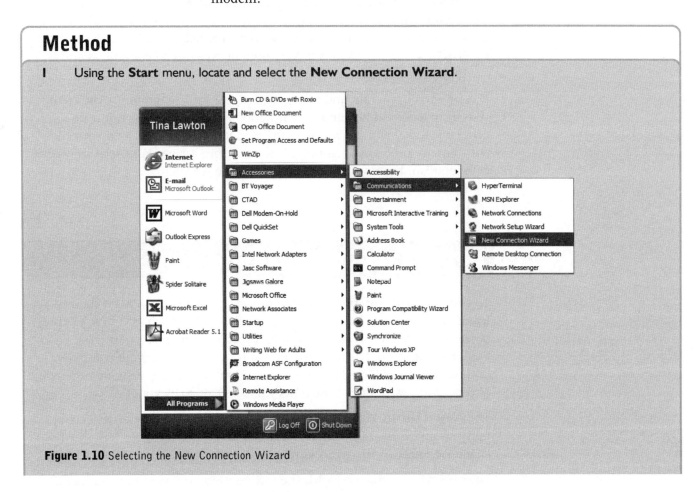

**Figure 1.10** Selecting the New Connection Wizard

## Information

Click on **Next** after completing each screen.

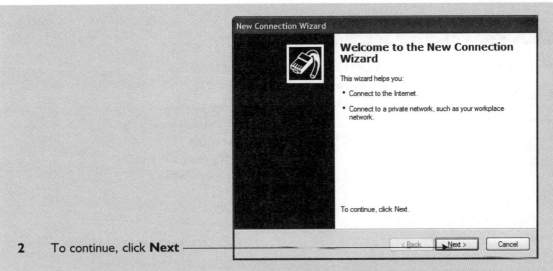

**2**    To continue, click **Next**

**Figure 1.11** The New Connection Wizard

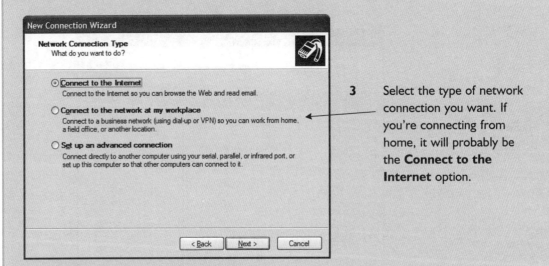

**3**    Select the type of network connection you want. If you're connecting from home, it will probably be the **Connect to the Internet** option.

**Figure 1.12** Selecting your network connection type

**4**    Select how you want to connect to the Internet. In this example, setting up the connection manually is shown, but you might choose the **Use the CD I got from an ISP** option if you have the CD to hand.

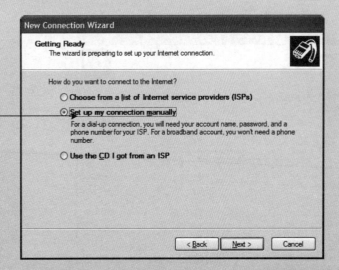

**Figure 1.13** Selecting how you want to set up your connection

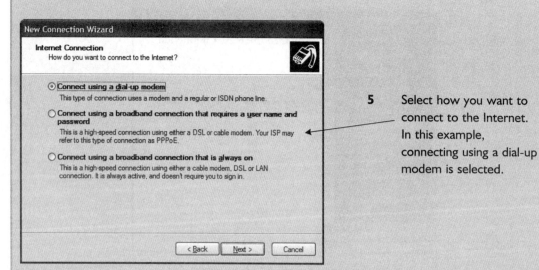

**Figure 1.14** Selecting how you want to connect to the Internet

5   Select how you want to connect to the Internet. In this example, connecting using a dial-up modem is selected.

6   Enter your ISP's name.

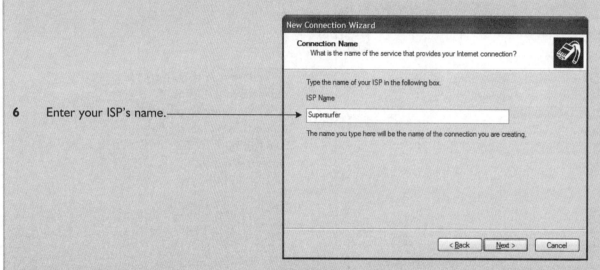

**Figure 1.15** Giving your connection a name

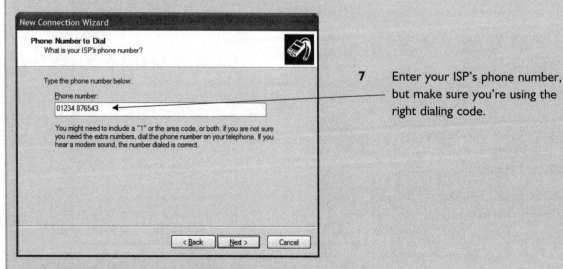

7   Enter your ISP's phone number, but make sure you're using the right dialing code.

**Figure 1.16** Entering your ISP's phone number

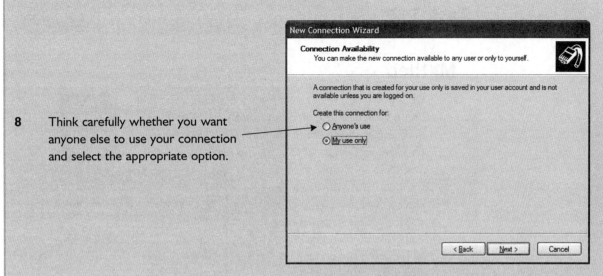

**8** Think carefully whether you want anyone else to use your connection and select the appropriate option.

**Figure 1.17** Selecting who can use the connection

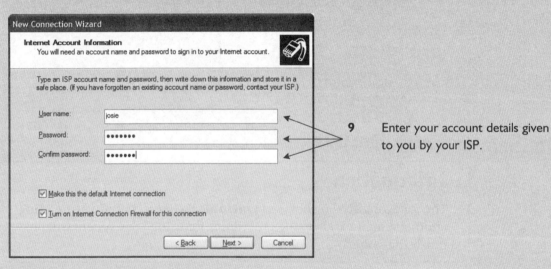

**9** Enter your account details given to you by your ISP.

**Figure 1.18** Entering user name and password

**10** You can now connect to your ISP and will soon be able to start sending e-mails.

**Figure 1.19** Completing the New Connection Wizard

## Method

1   Double click on the **Outlook Express** icon, which will be on your desktop, or click the icon on the taskbar or in the programs menu (if you have a different e-mail package, you will need to open this program instead).

2   The **Dial-up Connection** box will open. You now have the choice of connecting to your service provider, by entering your password and username as required, and clicking on **Connect**, or, by selecting **Work Offline** you can compose your e-mails without running up call charges.

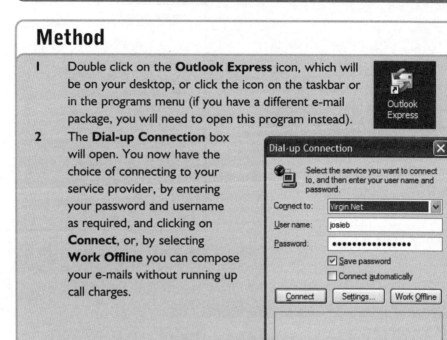

**Figure 1.20** Choosing how to connect to your ISP

## Information

The following screen shots use **Outlook Express**, but if you are using another e-mail package, the procedures for using your system will be much the same.

You will find a window similar to the one shown below:

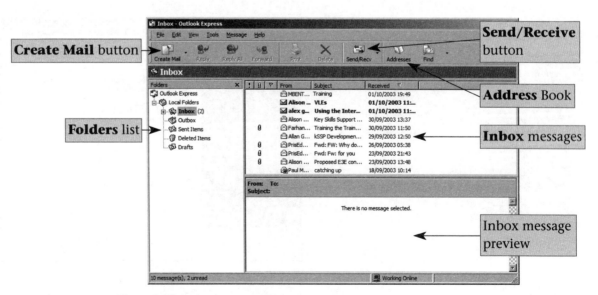

**Figure 1.21** Outlook Express window

- **Folders list**   This shows all the folders and subfolders in which your e-mails are stored.
- **Inbox messages**   This shows a list of all the messages in your Inbox. You can use the options menus to decide where your incoming messages are sent, but the Inbox is the default (original set-up) folder for incoming messages.
- **Inbox messages preview**   The contents of the selected message will be shown here.

## The Outlook Express toolbar

The toolbar provides access to some of the main functions, including sending and receiving e-mails, printing them and deleting messages.

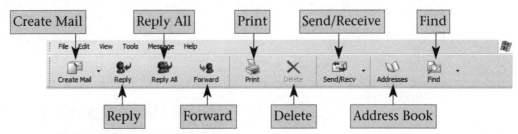

**Figure 1.22** Toolbar functions

- **Create Mail**     This opens a blank e-mail message window.
- **Reply**           Click on this to reply to any selected message in your Inbox. A new message window opens with the address already entered in the **To:** box. You can choose to have the message copied in your reply.
- **Reply All**       You can reply to a message and send it to all the others who have received the same message.
- **Forward**         This button allows you to forward any message to someone else by filling in the appropriate address in the **To:** box.
- **Print**           If you want a copy of your e-mail, click on this button.
- **Delete**          You can tidy up your folders by deleting any selected messages you no longer want.
- **Send/Recv**       This will send any messages in your **Outbox** and check for new mail (assuming you're online).
- **Addresses**       To open your address book, use this button.
- **Find**            This button will open a dialogue box to allow you to search for a message.

In the folders list you will have:

- **Inbox**           This is where the messages you receive are stored.
- **Outbox**          This is where messages you are sending are stored.
- **Sent Items**      This folder stores the messages you have sent.
- **Deleted Items**   This is where any messages you have deleted are stored.
- **Drafts**          This is where messages you are still working on are stored.

If you click on a folder, it will show you all the messages stored inside it.

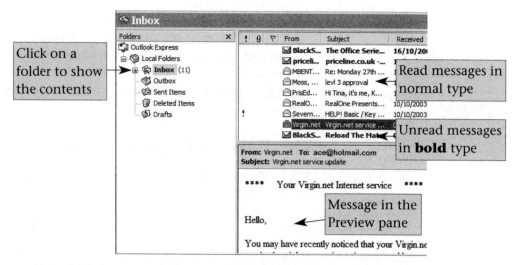

**Figure 1.23** E-mail messages in the Inbox folder

## Task 1.3 — Closing your e-mail program and disconnecting from your ISP

## Method

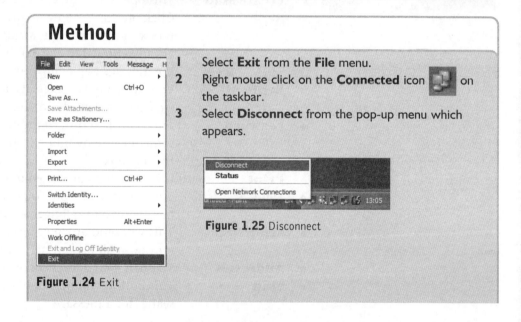

1 Select **Exit** from the **File** menu.
2 Right mouse click on the **Connected** icon on the taskbar.
3 Select **Disconnect** from the pop-up menu which appears.

**Figure 1.24** Exit

**Figure 1.25** Disconnect

## Task 1.4 — Setting up a new e-mail account

If you already have an e-mail address or want to create a new account, you will need to have the following information:
- Your display name.
- Your e-mail address.
- The addresses of your ISP's mail servers.
- Your account name and password.

# Method

1    Open Outlook Express.
2    Select **Accounts** from the **Tools** menu.
3    Under the **Mail** tab, select **Add** and then **Mail** from the pop-up menu.
4    Enter the details requested in the following boxes, clicking **Next** to move through the screens.
5    Click on **Finish** when all details have been entered.

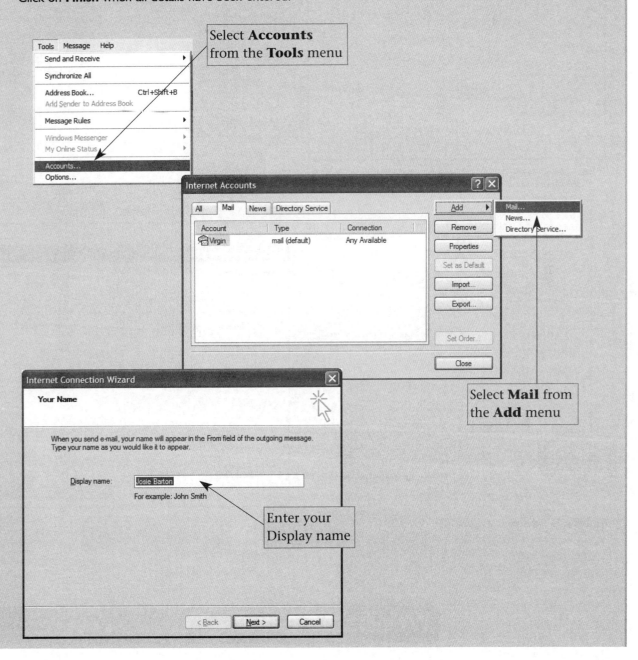

Select **Accounts** from the **Tools** menu

Select **Mail** from the **Add** menu

Enter your Display name

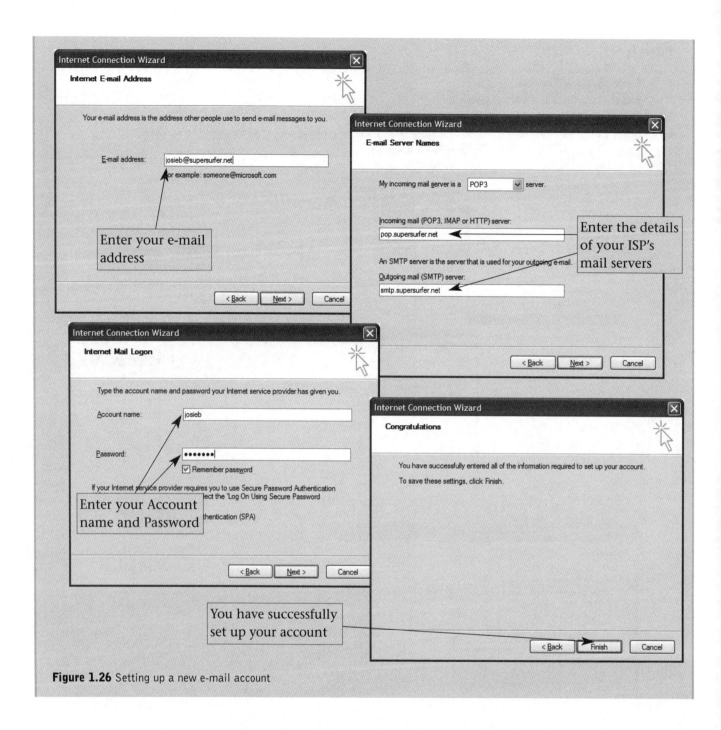

**Figure 1.26** Setting up a new e-mail account

## Web-based e-mail

With Outlook Express and other e-mail programs loaded onto your computer, you can compose your e-mails when you are offline and just connect to the Net to send (and check) your mail. This saves considerable money in call charges but can be a problem if you need to check your mail when you are away from home. You can certainly connect to your ISP wherever you may be, but can you imagine the call cost if you were sunning yourself on a tropical beach? This is when web-based e-mail can be a good option. Instead of using a dedicated e-mail program, you can create a free account with a web-based e-mail service such as Hotmail or Excite mail.

You'll have a new e-mail address which will be similar to josie@hotmail.com. Being web-based, you can read and write your e-mails by logging on to your e-mail service and entering your personal username and password. It then doesn't matter where you are in the world, you can still pick up your mail and reply using any of the cyber cafés or hotel Internet facilities that can be found all over the globe. It can be very useful to have both an e-mail facility provided by your ISP and a web-based e-mail address, but you will have to make sure that people know which one to use and when to use it if you are going away.

There are a couple of disadvantages to using web-based e-mail, however. You still need a way of connecting to the Internet, probably provided by an ISP, you have to be online to read and write your e-mails, which could soon mount up to quite a cost in call charges, and you can only read your e-mails while you are online. Once you disconnect from the Internet, as your e-mails stay on the provider's server, you cannot then quickly check a message's contents when you've forgotten some detail, without re-connecting.

| Task 1.5 | Creating a web-based e-mail account (using Hotmail for this example) |
|---|---|

## Method

1    Connect to the Internet.
2    Load the web page for Hotmail at www.hotmail.com.
3    Complete the form with your details.
4    **Sign in**.

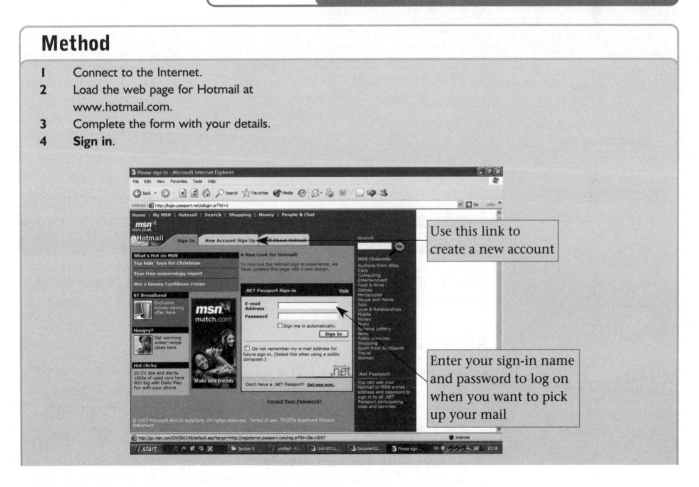

Use this link to create a new account

Enter your sign-in name and password to log on when you want to pick up your mail

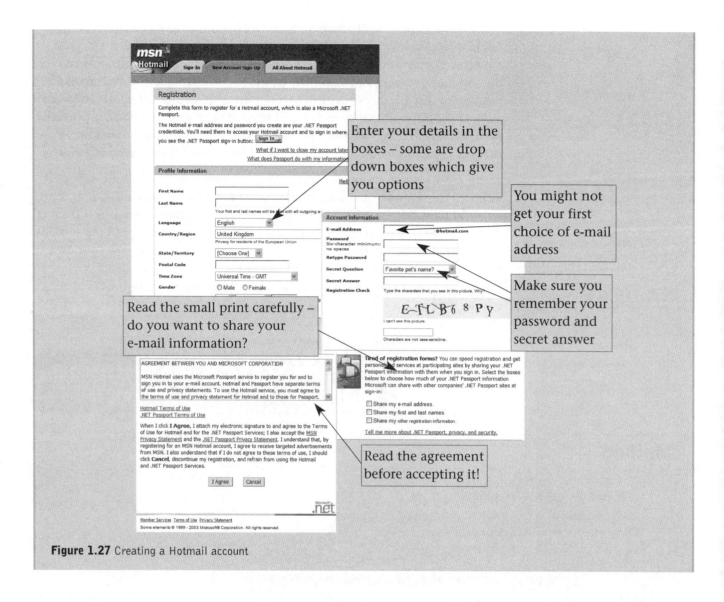

**Figure 1.27** Creating a Hotmail account

The figure contains the following annotations:

Enter your details in the boxes – some are drop down boxes which give you options

You might not get your first choice of e-mail address

Make sure you remember your password and secret answer

Read the small print carefully – do you want to share your e-mail information?

Read the agreement before accepting it!

# Pros and cons of using e-mail

E-mail is a quick, cheap way of keeping in touch with other people, but like any system, it has its good points and bad points.

## Advantages

- It is almost instantaneous. Mail is sent immediately you click the Send button without having to walk to the postbox or remember to buy a stamp. Your message should get to the recipient very shortly after it is sent and they can reply as soon as they check their e-mail box.
- E-mail is less formal than writing a letter. The whole idea of e-mail is that it is a brief, quick and direct way of communicating, so you wouldn't need to write reams. In fact, a lengthy e-mail might be difficult for some people to read and absorb onscreen. Many people feel that the odd spelling or punctuation error doesn't matter in an e-mail, although it's worth trying to proofread your e-mails quickly to see if you can spot errors or typos (typing errors). It makes it easier for the receiver to read if it's correct.

- You can reply to an e-mail without having to type in the recipient's address. If you reply to an e-mail, you can leave a copy of their message in your own e-mail so they don't have to search for the original message.
- It can be cheaper than sending a message by snail mail, especially taking into account that they will probably have the hardware and software already set up. You can send a message halfway across the world for the cost of a local phone call.
- You can keep in touch with friends and family very easily, and those who live in remote parts of the country don't feel quite so isolated if they are able to keep in touch.
- You can send documents and files as attachments, which can reach their destination quickly and safely. The recipient will have the files on their computer and can edit and return or forward them as necessary.

## Disadvantages

- You can only send an e-mail to someone who has a computer and an ISP account.
- E-mails may have a more casual approach than formal letters, but because people may not take the same care with an e-mail as they might do with an official letter, they can forget that an agreement by e-mail is just as legally binding as any formal document.
- You may find that junk mail (mail shots similar to the ones which come through your letter box on a regular basis!) can clutter up your Inbox, and, for that matter, take up precious room on your hard drive.
- There is always the risk of catching a virus from attachments. People distribute viruses to make mischief and, if they have access to a mailing list of e-mail addresses, may just send you an e-mail complete with a nasty surprise if you don't make a habit of virus checking all the attachments you receive.
- To communicate by e-mail is quick and easy, but it does depend on the recipient checking their Inbox regularly. If your e-mails remain on an ISP's server, then it's not really much help to you if you need a reply.

Can you think of any other advantages or disadvantages to add to this list?

# → Check your knowledge

1 Identify the functions of the buttons on the Outlook Express toolbar shown below.

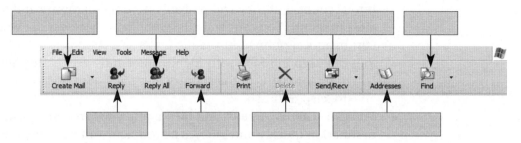

2 What are the advantages of web-based e-mail?

3 What equipment do you need to send e-mails?

4 Identify the components of this e-mail address:

# ace@college.ac.uk

5 What would you expect to find in:

   **a** Your Inbox.
   **b** Your Sent Items folder.
   **c** Your Deleted Items folder.

6 What are the two main protocols used by computers to move e-mails around?

7 What factors can affect the speed at which your e-mails are sent and received?

8 How can you tell which messages you have read from those you haven't read?

9 What services, other than e-mail, might an ISP offer?

10 Find out and note down the following:

- Your ISP's telephone number.
- Your username.
- Your e-mail address.
- The addresses of your ISP's mail servers.

# Section 2

## Sending e-mails

### You will learn to

- Write tactful e-mail messages and observe Internet etiquette
- Create and send e-mail messages
- Spellcheck e-mail messages
- Save e-mail messages
- Attach files to e-mail messages
- Compose e-mail messages in a word processing application
- Explain how hyperlinks can be inserted in a message
- Insert picture, attach stationery and attach signature to e-mail messages
- Send copies of e-mail messages to several people
- Print e-mail messages
- Identify security issues surrounding e-mails
- Create e-mails for sending later
- Find e-mail addresses

## Netiquette

There are very few rules about what you can or can't do on the Net, but there is a general agreement about what is considered good and bad manners. A code of conduct has grown through the increased use of the Net which is often referred to as Netiquette, and should be observed when you use e-mail.

**Rule 1**    Keep it brief. It is common sense to make sure that your e-mails are brief, clear and concise. It takes less time online to send and less time online to download. If you're paying your own phone bill, that could be quite a consideration, especially if you send and receive quite a few e-mails on a regular basis.

**Rule 2**    Watch what you say and how you say it! It isn't always easy with words on a page, especially written quickly and briefly, to communicate exactly what you want to say. On the phone, you can often tell what people **are not** saying by their tone of voice, but it's difficult to put that into a text message.

There are two ways of communicating feelings on the Net. One is by putting words in brackets to show a little about your mood, for example <grin>, <sob>. The other way is to use what's called **emoticons** or **smileys**. These are made up of keyboard characters and if you look at them sideways, they appear to be little faces with different expressions. Some examples of emoticons are:

| | | | |
|---|---|---|---|
| :-D | Laughing | :-( | Sad |
| :-) | Happy | :-/ | Confused |
| :-O | Shocked | ;-) | Wink |
| :'-) | Crying | :-l | Not amused |
| :-ll | Angry | >:-) | Evil grin |

There are, of course, many others used by people who send e-mails regularly.

**Rule 3**   Only use acronyms (where initial letters are used to make up another word, although strictly speaking these aren't acronyms but are commonly referred to as such) that others will understand. The use of acronyms in e-mail messages is popular because it cuts down the time spent online composing your message, and time costs money. The use of these acronyms has taken off with the increase in text messaging in recent years.

Some common acronyms are:

| | |
|---|---|
| **AFAIK** | As far as I know |
| **BCNU** | Be seeing you |
| **BTW** | By the way |
| **FYI** | For your information |
| **FAQ** | Frequently asked questions |
| **L8R** | See you later |
| **ROFL** | Rolls on the floor laughing |
| **TNX** | Thanks |

Again, there are many more and new ones are joining the list all the time.

**Rule 4**   Don't shout! ENTERING YOUR TEXT IN CAPITAL LETTERS DOESN'T LOOK VERY FRIENDLY, AND IS TAKEN AS SHOUTING.

**Rule 5**   Reply promptly. Because e-mail is so quick and easy, people generally expect a reply, even if it's only to say that you've received their e-mail.

**Rule 6**   Don't forward someone else's e-mail without their permission. After all, you wouldn't like anyone to do that to what you thought was a private message.

**Rule 7**   Following on from Rule 6, don't put anything in an e-mail that is confidential. Anyone can forward your e-mail to a newspaper, your boss at work, or your parents, so make a phone call to pass on your message if it's at all private.

**Remember:**

Although e-mail is a very quick and easy way to send messages, files and other data, and can often be written with a more casual style, any agreement made by e-mail can be just as legally binding.

Unlike a formal letter where you have to include addresses, a date and follow a fairly rigid format (not to mention having to remember the rules about whether you sign off faithfully or sincerely!), there are no set rules about how you lay out your message. You can start and end your messages to reflect your personality, although it's still worth thinking carefully about the recipient of your e-mail and the most appropriate format to use. As it is less formal than a letter, some people feel that spelling and punctuation are not as important, but an e-mail message with lots of errors is not only difficult to read, but doesn't look that good either, so it's always worth spending a couple of extra minutes proofreading it and using the spellchecker.

## Task 2.1 — Creating and sending an e-mail

### Hint:

Check your typing carefully – make sure you haven't left any spaces in the address or left out any of the full stops.

### Hint:

You can use the spellchecking button to check that you haven't made any spelling errors.

## Method

1. Click on the **Create Mail** button
2. The **New Message** window will appear.
3. Click in the **To:** box, and type in the e-mail address of the person you are sending the message to.
4. Click in the **Subject:** box, and type in a word or short sentence to indicate what the message is about.
5. Click in the message section underneath, and type in your message.
6. Click on the **Send** button

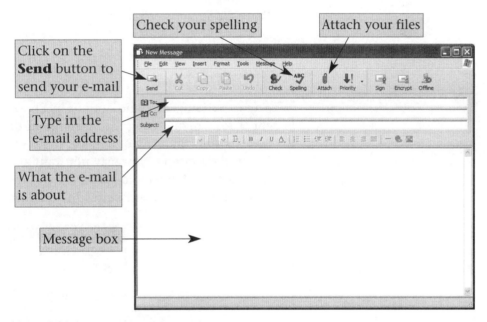

**Figure 2.1** Sending an e-mail

If you are using an internal network, your message will be sent straight away. This will also happen if your network has a permanent connection to the phone system or to an ISDN line. A copy of the message will be placed in your **Sent Items** folder. If you don't want to send your message straight away, you can select the **Send Later** option from the File menu.

If you have prepared your message **offline** (not connected) your message will be placed in your **Outbox** folder. It will remain there until you connect to your ISP and click on the **Send and Receive All** button

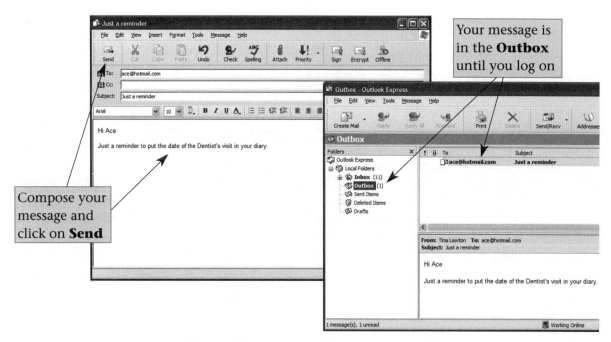

Your message is in the **Outbox** until you log on

Compose your message and click on **Send**

**Figure 2.2** Sending an e-mail later

## Information

You can change the send options by choosing the **Options** item from the **Tools** menu. Using the **Send** tab in the dialogue box which appears you can select or deselect items by clicking in the appropriate boxes. For example, you may not want a copy of your message placed in your **Sent Items** folder and you would uncheck the box next to the **Save copy of sent messages in the 'Sent Items' folder**.

You can change the settings for Outlook Express using this **Options** dialogue box

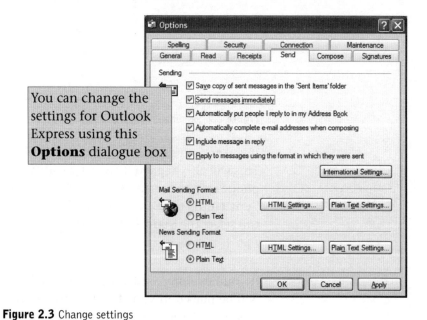

**Figure 2.3** Change settings

## Information

If your message is urgent, you can also change the priority of the message by selecting the **Priority** button on the toolbar. A high priority message will have an exclamation mark against it when it is received.

Set the priority of the message: **High** if it's urgent, or **Low** if it can wait

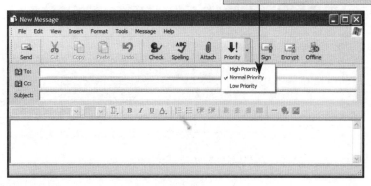

**Figure 2.4** Setting the priority of a message

## → Practise your skills 1

1 Open your e-mail program.

2 Start a new message.

3 Enter the e-mail address of someone you know or your tutor.

4 Enter 'Sending e-mail' in the **Subject** box.

5 Type in this message: 'I am sending you this e-mail message as one of my practice tasks for my City & Guilds E-mail Unit. Please let me know that it has reached you safely.'

6 Send the message. (If you are working offline you will need to connect to your ISP.)

7 Close your e-mail program.

| Task 2.2 | Spellchecking your e-mail |
|----------|---------------------------|

## Method

1 Click on the **Spelling** button **ABC ✓ Spelling** or choose the **Spelling** option from the **Tools** menu.

2 Check any words which are highlighted by the spellchecker and click on **Change** or **Ignore** the suggestion.

3 Click on **OK** when the **spelling check is complete** dialogue box appears.

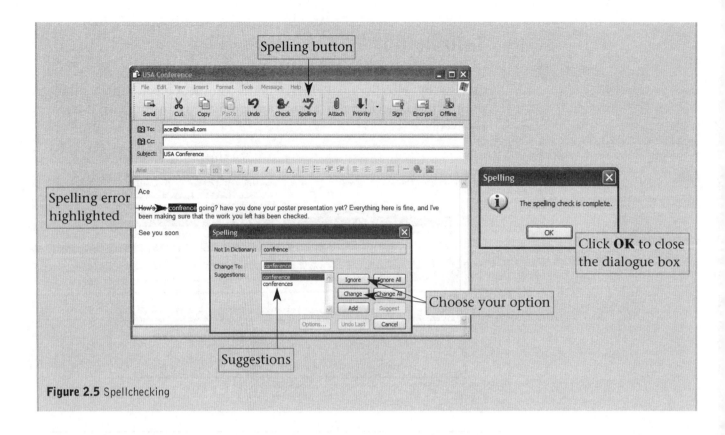

**Figure 2.5** Spellchecking

**Hint:**

You can set your options to spellcheck your e-mails before sending them by selecting **Options** from the **Tools** menu.

## Information

Outlook Express shares a dictionary with the **Word** program, so you will need this installed on your computer to use the spellcheck function.

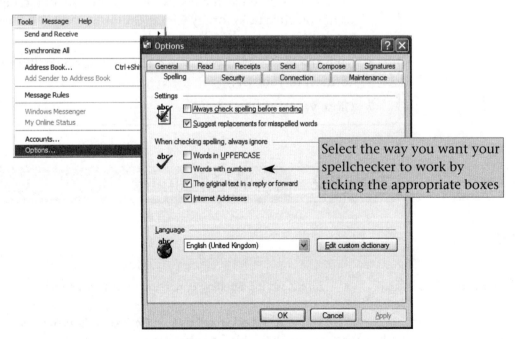

**Figure 2.6** Setting options to spellcheck

## The Message toolbar

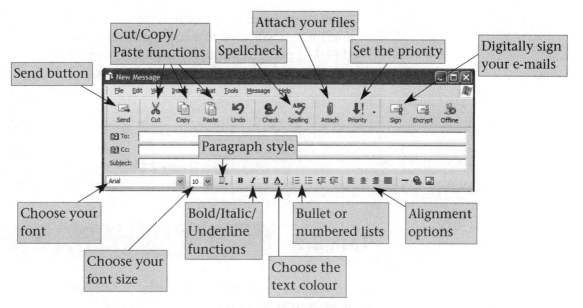

**Figure 2.7** The Message toolbar

**Font**   You can select the font type you would like to use in your e-mail using this drop down list box. The screen shot shows the **Arial** font is selected.

**Font size**   Select the size of font using the drop down list box. The screen shot shows that the font size selected is 10.

**Bold, Underline, Italic**   Select these options to format the text in your e-mail.

**Paragraph style**   Select options from this drop down list to choose the format of your paragraphs, e.g. headings, bulleted lists, numbered lists.

**Text colour**   To add a bit of colour to your message you can select the colour from this palette. This can be useful if you are replying to a message to show the bits you're adding.

**Bulleted or numbered lists**   Useful if you want to be brief and put your points down in a list rather than text.

**Alignment**   Justify, right and left align, and centre your text using these options.

**Spellcheck**   If you're not sure about your spelling – use this option to check it.

**Attach**   This will allow you to attach a file to your e-mail.

**Priority**   If your message is urgent, you can set this option to high priority.

**Sign**   This will allow you to digitally sign your e-mails.

## Information

To use these formatting functions in your e-mail program you will need to select the **Rich Text (HTML)** option from the **Format** menu, otherwise your e-mail message will just be **Plain Text**.

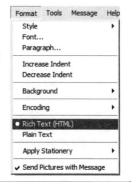

**Figure 2.8** Rich Text (HMTL)

---

| Task 2.3 | Saving e-mails |

Having written your e-mail, you might want to save it as a file so that you can open it in another program.

## Method

| | |
|---|---|
| I | Click on the **Sent Items** folder. |
| 2 | Select the message you want to save. |
| 3 | Select the **Save As** option from the **File** menu. |
| 4 | Enter a name for the file in the **Save As** dialogue box or accept the suggestion. |
| 5 | Select the **Save as type** from the drop down list box. |
| 6 | Choose where you will save the file. |
| 7 | Click on **Save**. |

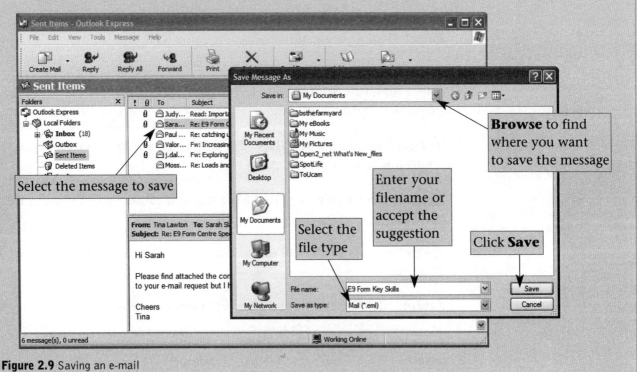

**Figure 2.9** Saving an e-mail

## Task 2.4 — Using e-mail attachments

You can **attach** files and documents to your e-mail, which makes it very useful if you want to get your documents to someone more quickly (and often more cheaply) than snail mail. Attachments can include word processed documents, images, sound or video files, and even computer programs. When you send an attachment, your mail program copies the file from wherever it is located and attaches it to your message. You can send more than one file as an attachment, in fact you could send a word processed document and an image and a video clip with the same e-mail – but be warned, an image file might take quite a while to send, and to receive. You may not be too popular with your friends if you keep sending them large files which mean they have to stay online for quite a while waiting for the files to download!

## Method

1   Load your e-mail program.
2   Click on the **Create Mail** button on the toolbar.
3   Enter the e-mail address, the subject and your message.

4   Click on the **Attach File** button  on the toolbar.
    Attach

5   The **Insert Attachment** window appears.
6   Select the drive where the file you wish to send has been saved.
7   Click on the file, so that it appears in the **File name:** box.
8   Click on **Attach**.
9   Your file will be shown in the **Attach:** box of your message.
10  **Send** the e-mail.

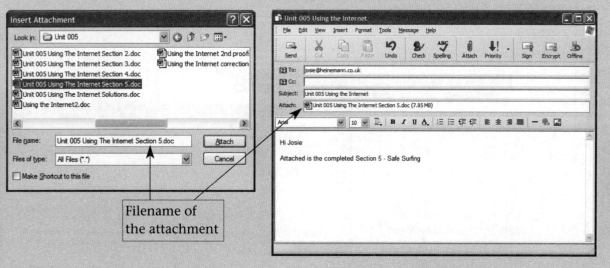

**Figure 2.10** Attaching a file to an e-mail

## Information

You may find that you want to delete an attachment because you've made a mistake and attached the wrong file prior to sending an e-mail. Simply select the file icon in the message header and press **Delete** on the keyboard. Now you can try again, and attach the file you really wanted to send!

| Task 2.5 | Composing an e-mail in a word processing program |
|---|---|

Entering text directly into your e-mail program is just one way of creating a message. You can also compose your e-mail in a word processing application, such as **Word**, and then copy the text into the message window.

## Method

1. Load your word processing application.
2. Enter the text of your message.
3. Highlight the text you want to include in your e-mail message and **Copy** it. (**Remember:** Use **Edit/Copy** or **Ctrl + C**.)
4. Load your e-mail program.
5. Start a new e-mail message.
6. **Paste** the text into the message section of a new e-mail message. (**Remember:** Use **Edit/Paste** or **Ctrl + V**.)
7. Add any other text you may want to include and send the message in the normal way.

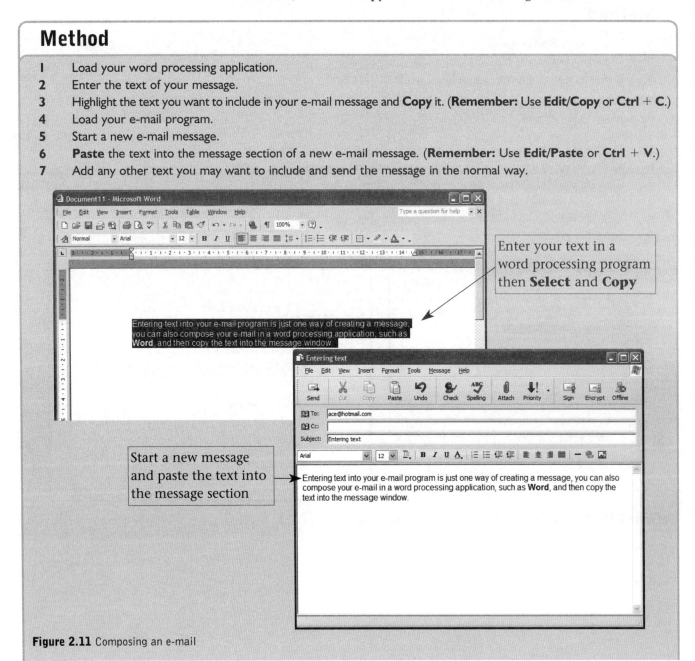

Enter your text in a word processing program then **Select** and **Copy**

Start a new message and paste the text into the message section

**Figure 2.11** Composing an e-mail

## Information

You can also select parts of a document to copy from your word processing program into an e-mail message, it doesn't have to be the whole thing. This can be a very useful option if you have a document already produced and just want to send selected parts of it to someone else.

| Task 2.6 | Inserting hyperlinks in an e-mail message |
|---|---|

**Remember:**

A hyperlink is used to jump from one web page to another. Hyperlinks can be images or underlined text.

One of the benefits of using e-mail to send information to people is that you don't always have to send them the information within your message. If you find something on a web page that you want to tell people about, you can simply insert the **hyperlink** into your e-mail message and they will be able to click on the link and open the web page.

## Method

1  Select **Hyperlink** from the **Insert** menu.
2  Enter the URL (Uniform Resource Locator – the web page address) into the dialogue box.
3  Click on **OK**.

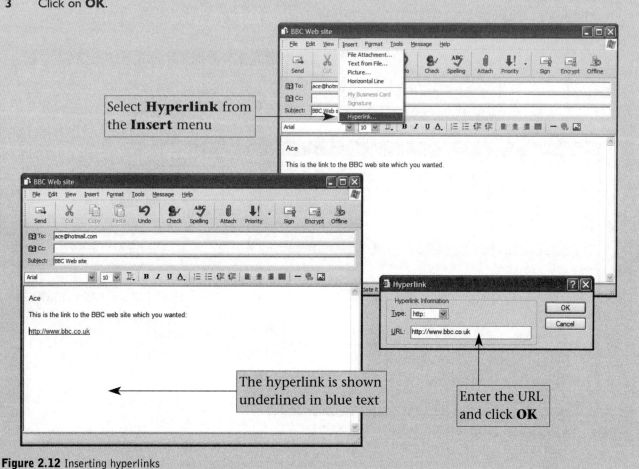

Select **Hyperlink** from the **Insert** menu

The hyperlink is shown underlined in blue text

Enter the URL and click **OK**

**Figure 2.12** Inserting hyperlinks

## Task 2.7 — Inserting a picture in an e-mail message

You can attach an image as a file using the method shown earlier in this section, but you can also insert the image into the body of your message.

## Method

1  Select **Picture** from the **Insert** menu.
2  Select **Browse** from the **Picture** dialogue box.
3  Browse your folders to find the picture you want to insert and select the file.
4  Click on **Open**.
5  The file location will be inserted in the **Picture** dialogue box. Click on the **OK** button.
6  The picture will be inserted in your e-mail message.

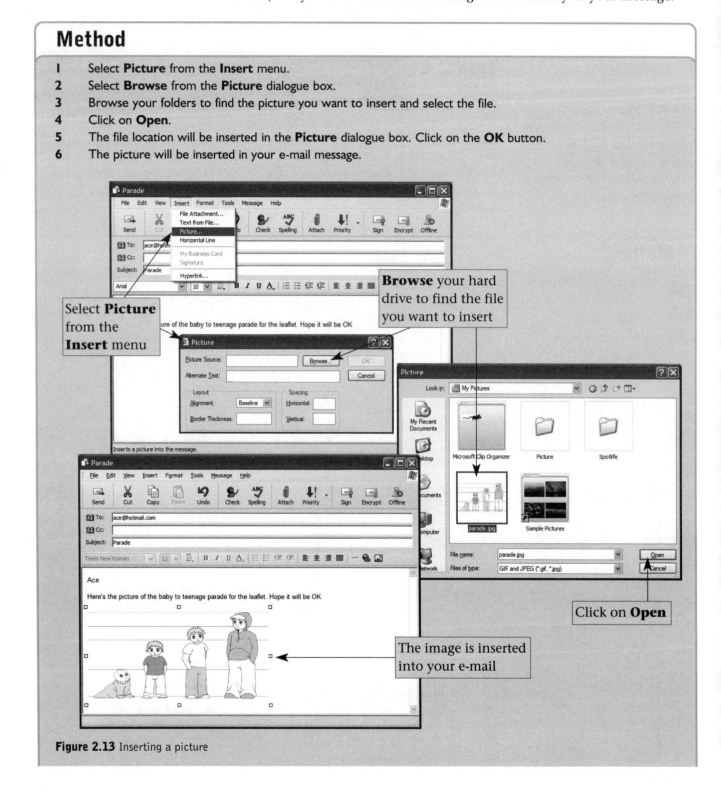

Select **Picture** from the **Insert** menu

**Browse** your hard drive to find the file you want to insert

Click on **Open**

The image is inserted into your e-mail

**Figure 2.13** Inserting a picture

Outlook Express comes with a selection of stationery designs to add a bit of colour and interest to your e-mails.

## Method

1 Select **Apply Stationery** from the **Format** menu.
2 Select the stationery design from the options.
3 Write your message and send as normal.

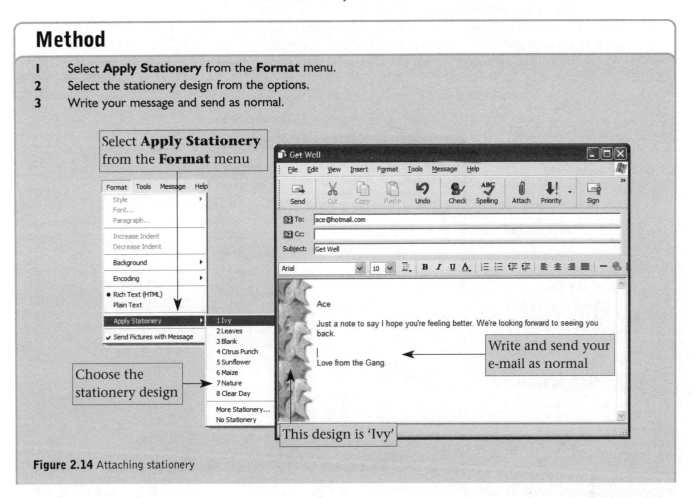

**Figure 2.14** Attaching stationery

Stationery is only a good idea if your recipient's e-mail program can display it.

You can add a short piece of text, such as a favourite quote or your work details, to your e-mail message using the **Signature** function.

## Information

You can have your signature automatically inserted into all your messages by selecting the **Add signatures to all outgoing mail** box in the **Options/Signature** box.

# Method

1 Select **Options** from the **Tools** menu.
2 Select the **Signature** tab in the **Options** box.
3 Select **New**.
4 Click on **Rename** to give your signature a name.
5 Select **Text** and enter the text you want to use as your signature.
6 Click on **Apply** to finish.
7 When you complete a message and want to add your signature, select **Signature** from the **Insert** menu.

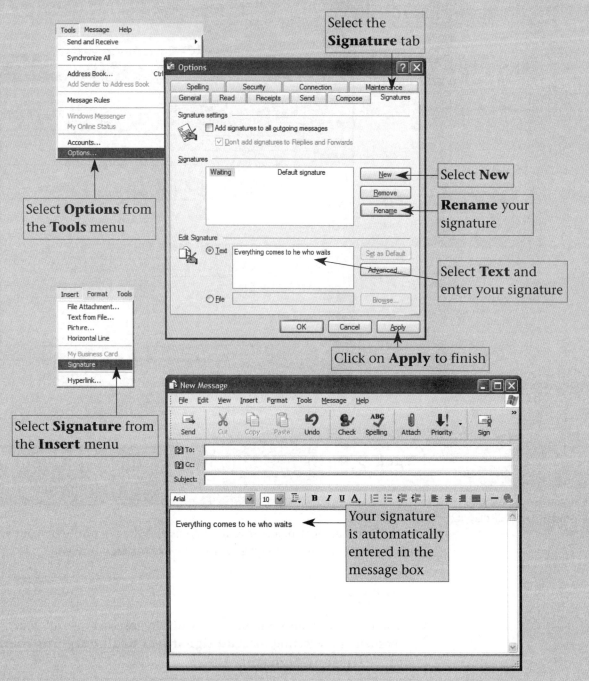

**Figure 2.15** Attaching your signature

## Task 2.10 | Sending a message to several people

You can send one message to several people at the same time by entering all the e-mail addresses in the **To:** box.

### Method

1 Click on the **Create Mail** button.
2 Enter the e-mail addresses of the people to whom you want to send the e-mail in the **To:** box separated by a comma or a semi-colon (;).
3 Complete and send your message in the normal way.

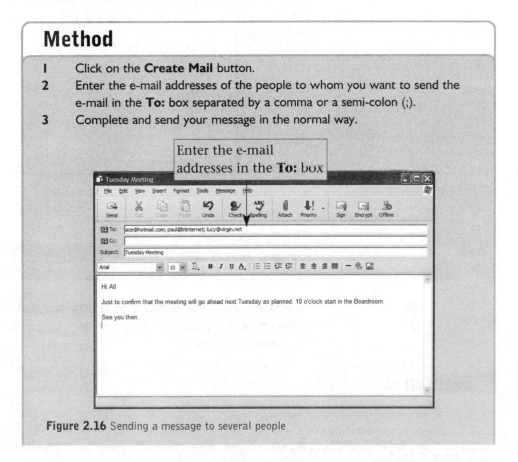

Enter the e-mail addresses in the **To:** box

**Figure 2.16** Sending a message to several people

## Task 2.11 | Sending a copy of a message

If you want to send a copy of your e-mail to someone else, you can use the **Cc:** box to enter the appropriate e-mail address.

### Method

1 Click on the **Create Mail** button.
2 Enter in the **Address** box the e-mail address of the person to whom you are sending the message.
3 Click in the **Cc:** box and enter the e-mail address of the person to whom you are sending a copy of the message.
4 Complete and send your message in the normal way.

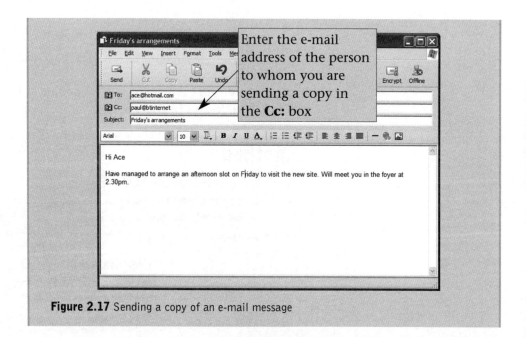

**Figure 2.17** Sending a copy of an e-mail message

## Task 2.12 | Sending a blind carbon copy

If you are sending a message to one person, but want to send a copy to someone else without that person knowing, you can use the **Bcc: (Blind Carbon Copy)** option.

## Method

1. Click on the **Create Mail** button.
2. Enter in the **Address** box the e-mail address of the person to whom you are sending the message.
3. Select **All Headers** from the **View** menu. A new box will appear below the **Cc:** box.
4. Click in the **Bcc:** box and enter the e-mail address of the person to whom you are sending a copy of the message.
5. Complete and send your message in the normal way.

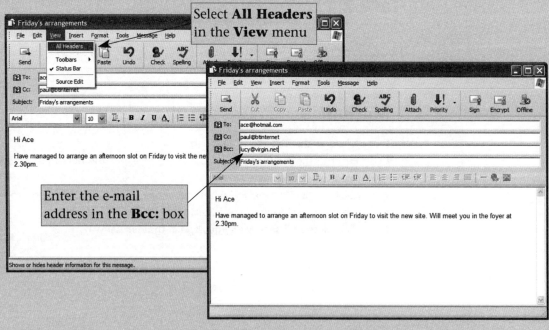

**Figure 2.18** Sending a blind carbon copy

## → Practise your skills 2

1 Open your e-mail program.

2 Start a new message.

3 Enter the e-mail address of someone you know or your tutor.

4 Compose an e-mail message and enter a title in the **Subject** box.

5 Enter your own e-mail address in the **Cc:** box.

6 **Send** the message. (If you are working offline you will need to connect to your ISP.)

7 Close your e-mail program.

## → Practise your skills 3

1 Open your e-mail program.

2 Start a new message.

3 Enter the e-mail addresses of someone you know *and* your tutor in the address box.

4 Compose an e-mail message and enter a title in the **Subject** box.

5 Enter your own e-mail address in the **Bcc:** box.

6 **Send** the message. (If you are working offline you will need to connect to your ISP.)

7 Close your e-mail program.

## Task 2.13  Printing e-mails

Sometimes you may want to print out a copy of an e-mail. Perhaps it contains information you need to complete a task, or instructions to go somewhere or do something.

## Method

1 Select the e-mail message you want to print.
2 Click on the **Print** button on the toolbar, or select **Print** from the **File** menu.
3 Check your printer settings.
4 Click on **OK**.

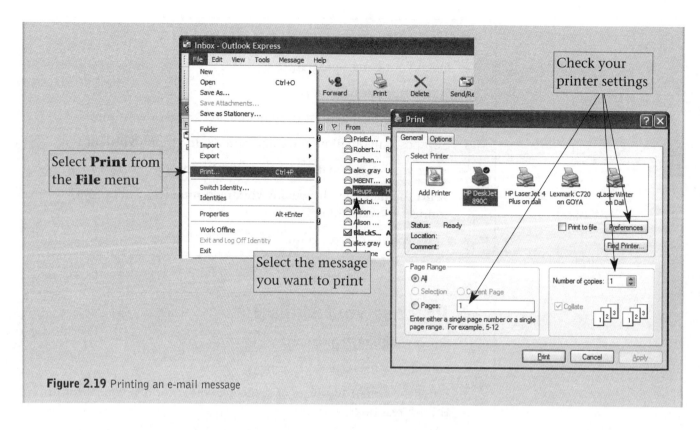

**Figure 2.19** Printing an e-mail message

When you print out your e-mail, you will notice that it contains more information than you see in the Message pane when you open it. You will find information such as the e-mail address or name of the sender, the e-mail address of you, the recipient, the date and time the e-mail was sent, and the subject of the e-mail.

There is usually a header and a footer on the printout which show the date the e-mail was printed out and the number of pages in the message.

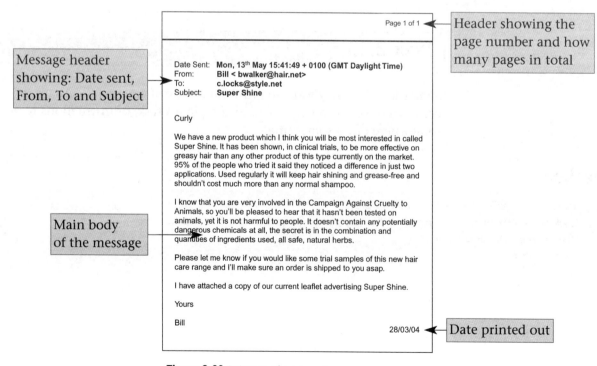

**Figure 2.20** Printout of an e-mail message

# E-mail security

## *Digital signatures*

As more people send information by e-mail, it is becoming increasingly important that your e-mails can't be read by anyone other than your recipient. A system to ensure that no one can pretend to be you and send information under your name which may be false or misleading is vital in today's business world. This can be done using **digital IDs** or **signatures**.

Using digital IDs in Outlook Express can prove your identity in electronic transactions, a bit like using your passport when you change foreign currency. You can also use a digital ID to encrypt (code) your e-mails to keep them from prying eyes as your recipient will need a key to the code to be able to read the message.

Digital IDs are issued by independent certification authorities, which will need to verify that you are who you say you are! You do this by completing a form on their web site with your personal details and they will then send you instructions on installing your digital ID. You can then use this to 'sign' your e-mails and ensure that your messages are secure.

## *Encryption*

E-mails are not really the most suitable way to send sensitive information which could be forwarded to almost anybody. If sensitive information has to be sent via e-mail, it may be better to use **encryption** to scramble it. Messages are encrypted and decrypted using two codes, called keys, that are entered into encryption software. One key is a private key, the other is a public key. You would pass on your public key to anyone who needed it and they would use it to encrypt the message being sent to you. You would then use your private key to decrypt the message when it reached you.

You can find out more about both these topics using the Outlook Express **Help** facility, or by selecting the **Security** option from the **Tools** menu.

**Figure 2.21** Encryption and digital signatures

In Section 1, the benefits of compiling e-mails offline in terms of cost savings were highlighted, but there are other advantages to writing your messages offline. Sometimes you may need to draft a message and perhaps think about it overnight, or you may be waiting for further information to complete the message, and, with the ever-increasing demands of work, you may find that you have only half completed your message and need to finish it off later. For any of these occasions, you can save the draft message in your **Drafts** folder, and then access the message again when it's convenient.

## Method

1   Start a new message.
2   Select **Save** from the **File** menu. Your message will be saved in the **Drafts** folder.
3   To complete the message double click on the message in the **Drafts** folder to open the message.
4   Complete and **Send** the message as normal.

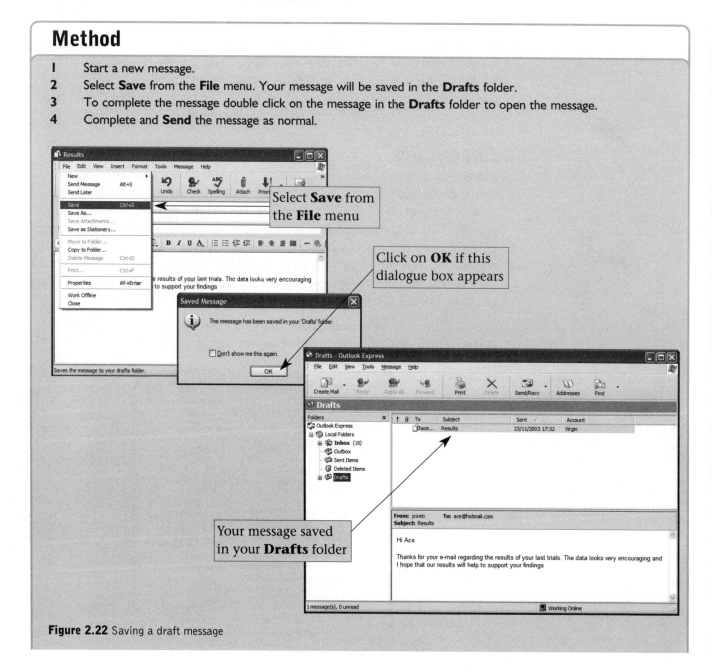

**Figure 2.22** Saving a draft message

| Task 2.15 | Finding e-mail addresses |
|---|---|

If you don't know someone's e-mail address, you may be able to find it using a **directory service**. A directory service is like a telephone directory for e-mail addresses, where you can search for a name to give you the e-mail address.

## Method

1 Select **People** from the **Find** option in the **Edit** menu.
2 Choose an address service from the drop down list box.
3 Enter the name of the person you wish to find.
4 Click on **Find Now**.
5 Outlook Express should connect to the Internet and search the directory chosen. A list of names will be displayed in the **Find People** box. Select the name you think is the one you need.
6 Click on **Close**.

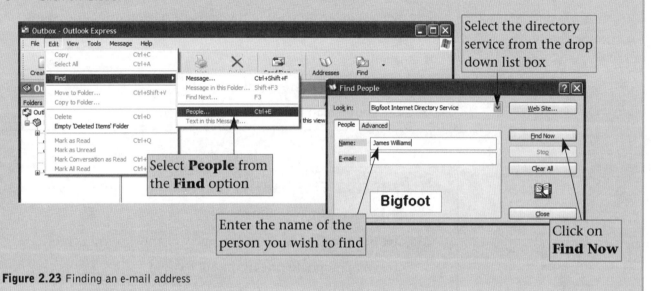

**Figure 2.23** Finding an e-mail address

## Information

You can access the **Find People** box from the Find button on the toolbar

## → Practise your skills 4

1 Open your word processing program and enter the following text:

'One of the benefits of using e-mail is that you can send messages to people quickly and easily. It will probably cost less than a first class stamp and you know it will reach their mail server in seconds rather than days. This means you can keep in touch with family and friends across the world.'

2 Save your file with the name **Keeping in touch**.

3 Open your e-mail program and enter your own e-mail address in the Address box.

4 Enter a suitable word or phrase in the Subject box.

5 Attach your file **Keeping in touch**.

6 Select and apply stationery suitable for a message to a friend.

7 Enter a suitable message in the message section using the **Arial** font.

8 Spellcheck your message.

9 Send the e-mail in the usual way.

10 Close your e-mail program and disconnect.


## → Practise your skills 5

1 Open your e-mail program.

2 Enter the e-mail address of someone you know or your tutor.

3 Enter an appropriate title in the Subject box.

4 Open your file **Keeping in touch** in your word processing program.

5 Select and copy the text.

6 Paste the text into the message section of your e-mail.

7 Add a message in the message section to explain why you are sending the message.

8 Select the text you have added and change the colour of the text to blue.

9 Set the message as High Priority.

10 Send the e-mail in the usual way.

11 Close your e-mail program and disconnect.

# → Practise your skills 6

1 Open your e-mail program.

2 Enter your own e-mail address in the Address box.

3 Enter the e-mail address of your tutor or a friend in the Cc: box.

4 Enter **Checking my signature** in the Subject box.

5 Create a signature which includes your name and a few words of a favourite quote.

6 Enter a suitable message in the message section and add your signature.

7 Send the e-mail in the usual way.

8 Close your e-mail program and disconnect.

# → Check your knowledge

1 If you wanted to send a copy of your message to someone without the recipient knowing, what function would you use?

2 What might you send as an attachment?

3 Why would you not send an e-mail message in capital letters?

4 What are the advantages of composing your messages offline?

5 Note down the stationery you have available in your e-mail program.

6 If you find you have attached the wrong file to an e-mail message, what would you do?

7 Identify the functions of the Outlook Express toolbar indicated by the blank boxes below:

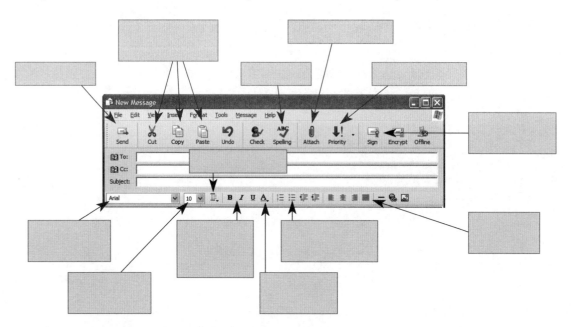

8 Why might people use digital signatures and/or encryption?

9 Why might you compose an e-mail message in a word processing program?

10 How could you find the e-mail address of someone using a directory service?

# Consolidation 1

1 Connect to the Internet and load the site www.bbc.co.uk.

2 Identify an image which you like and save it to your hard drive with a suitable name.

3 Open your e-mail program, enter the e-mail address of your tutor and a friend and a suitable subject title.

4 Insert your own e-mail address in the Bcc: box.

5 Enter the following text in the message section:

'I am inserting the URL of the BBC web site where I found the picture of *(insert the subject of your picture)* so that you can have a look at it. The URL is *(insert URL of the BBC web site)*. I am inserting the picture for you to see, and attaching it as a file so that you can save it if you like it.'

6 Centre your text.

7 Embolden the subject of your picture.

8 Insert the image into your message.

9 Attach the image file you saved.

10 Send your e-mail in the usual way.

11 Save your e-mail to your hard drive with a suitable filename.

12 Print out a copy of the e-mail.

13 Close your e-mail program and disconnect from the Internet.

## You will learn to

- Identify more than one type of view to read messages
- Open and read e-mail messages
- Describe what to do when a message is received
- Save messages
- Describe precautions to take when processing attachments
- View file attachments
- Save file attachments
- Print attached files
- Delete e-mail messages
- Forward e-mail messages to one person
- Forward e-mail messages to several people
- Edit received messages
- View message details
- Download files
- Identify the implications of downloading files
- Block messages from particular senders
- Use automated reply methods to respond to e-mail messages
- Describe potential problems of using automated reply involving many people

## Choosing your view

You can change the way Outlook Express looks by using the **Layout** option in the **View** menu. In the screen shot below, the Preview pane is shown. Using this layout will enable you to see the message selected in the Preview pane, although you can read the message in a separate window by double clicking on the e-mail in the message list.

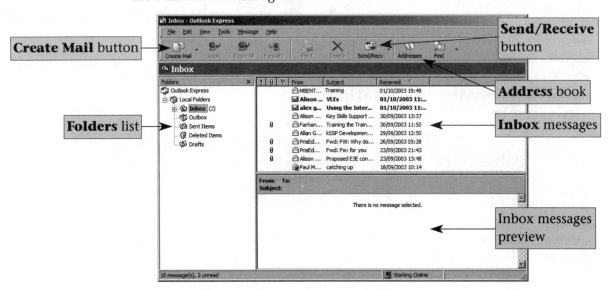

**Figure 3.1** Previewing an e-mail message

## Method

1    Select **Layout** from the **View** menu.
2    Check the options you want to use for your layout.
3    Click on **Apply** and then **OK** to close the box and implement the changes.

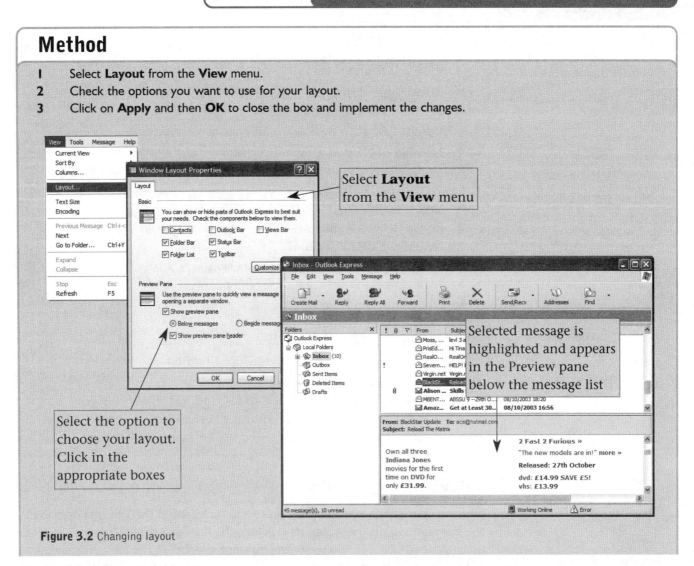

**Figure 3.2** Changing layout

Task 3.2　　Receiving an e-mail

When an e-mail message is received it is placed in your **Inbox** folder.

## Method

1    Load your e-mail program and connect to your ISP.
2    Click on the **Send and Receive All** button.
3    Any incoming messages will be placed in your **Inbox** folder.
4    Click on the **Inbox** folder.
5    Select the new message to read it.

## Information

Your new messages will appear in your Inbox in **bold** type. This changes to a regular typeface when the message has been read.

Click on a folder to show the contents

Read messages in normal type

Unread messages in **bold** type

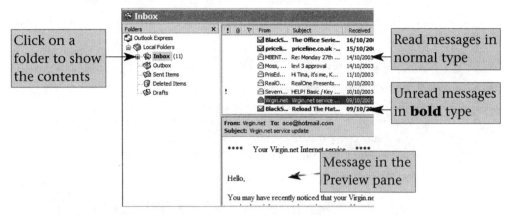

Message in the Preview pane

**Figure 3.3** Receiving an e-mail

## Information

You can select the message and read it in the Preview pane, or double click on the message and it will open in a separate window as shown below:

This message header gives all the details about the message: From, To, Subject and Date

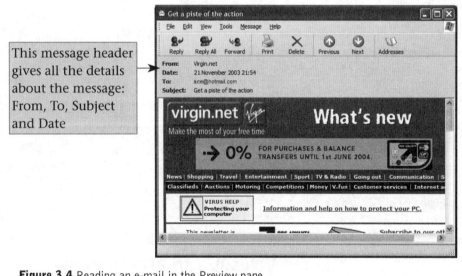

**Figure 3.4** Reading an e-mail in the Preview pane

When you have received your e-mail messages and read them, you can then decide what you need to do. Perhaps you want to print out a copy for future reference, or save it to your hard drive. You will also need to think about replying to the message and whether you need to forward it to someone else. Having read your message, you may not need to keep it any longer and can then delete it. Receiving your messages is just the first step!

Having received your e-mails, you might want to save an e-mail as a file so that you can open it in another program.

## Method

1  Click on the **Inbox** folder.
2  Select the message you want to save.
3  Select the **Save As** option from the **File** menu.
4  Enter a name for the file in the **Save As** dialogue box or accept the suggestion.
5  Select the **Save as type** from the drop down list box.
6  Choose where you will save the file.
7  Click on **Save**.

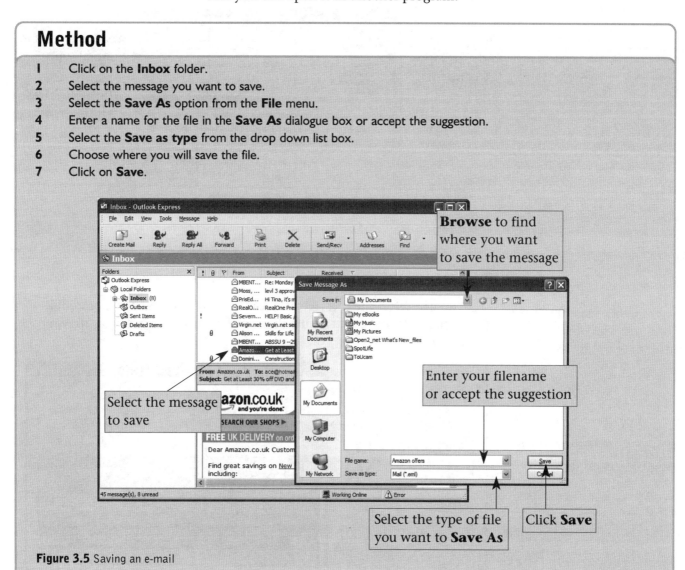

**Figure 3.5** Saving an e-mail

## Viruses and attachments

A **virus** is a small piece of code deliberately buried inside a program to cause mischief. When the program is run, the virus starts running too. Some viruses are written as a joke to display a message on your screen or make your computer beep every now and then, but others can do a lot of damage to the data in your files and even erase all the information on your hard drive. There are thousands of different viruses and new ones are being invented all the time. The software which can find and clean out a virus is called **anti-virus** software.

Viruses can be distributed across the Internet in several ways:

- Software downloaded from the Internet may have a virus. This could be from software which has been illegally copied (usually called pirated software) or shareware which has been infected.
- Viruses can be transmitted by an e-mail attachment. A plain text e-mail is harmless, but a file sent with the e-mail as an attachment could carry a virus. You should always be suspicious of an e-mail attachment from someone you don't know, but if a friend's computer is infected, they might send you an attachment which hides a virus without realising it.
- A macro virus is a type of computer virus that is hidden inside a macro in a document, template, or add-in. A macro is a recorded set of actions which can be replayed to save time, such as changing fonts in Word (you can assign a hotkey to a macro, similar to Ctrl + V to paste into a document). Any documents with a macro virus that you download from the Internet can infect your computer and, if you send the document to others, it can infect their computers too.

The only safeguard against infecting your machine is to use an anti-virus utility which you should **update** and **use** regularly. Run your virus checker to scan any files you download or receive *before* you open them, to be on the safe side.

## Receiving e-mail attachments

E-mails can be sent to you with an attachment. An attachment is a file: it could be a document, an image, a video or music clip, or a program. You will need to take great care opening any such files you receive as they can carry viruses. It is important to scan any e-mail attachment with a virus checker before you open it.

When you receive an attachment, the message is displayed in the message list with a paper clip icon next to it. You will have two choices: to save it as a file or to open it.

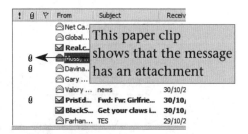

**Figure 3.6** An attachment

## Information

The icons shown in the Message pane can give you information about the messages:

✉ Your message has not been read

✉ Your message has been read

✉ You have replied to the message

## Method 1

1   In the Preview pane, your attachment will be shown as a paper clip in the top right-hand corner of the pane.
2   Click on the paper clip and you will see the filename and an option to save the attachment.
3   Click on the filename and the **Open Attachment Warning** dialogue box appears. Select the **Open it** option and it will open, provided you have a program on your computer which will open files of the type sent!
4   View the attachment and then close your program in the usual way.

Click on the paper clip in the Preview pane

Select the option you want

Select **Open it** if you're sure it's OK.

**Level 3 Certificate in Adult Literacy Subject Support**

*Scheme handbook*

This will open the document with the appropriate program

**Figure 3.7** Opening an attachment

## Method 2

1   Double click on the message in the message list.
2   Double click on the file attachment in the message header.
3   Select the **Open it** option from the **Open Attachment Warning** dialogue box. This will open the file in the appropriate program.
4   View the attachment and then close your program in the usual way.

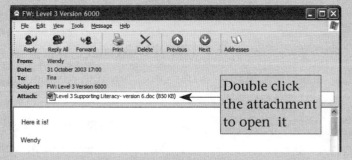

Double click the attachment to open it

**Figure 3.8** Another method of opening an attachment

### Remember:

Although there are often scare stories about viruses being spread by e-mails, a plain text e-mail won't carry a virus – it's only the attachments which do that. That's why it is so important to virus check any attachments you receive *before* you open them.

You may want to save your attachments to your hard disk and look at them later.

## Method 1

1 In the Preview pane, your attachment will be shown as a paper clip in the top right-hand corner of the pane.
2 Click on the paper clip and you will see the filename and an option to save the attachment.
3 Click on the **Save Attachments** option.
4 Browse your hard drive to find where you want to save your attachment, and click **Save**.

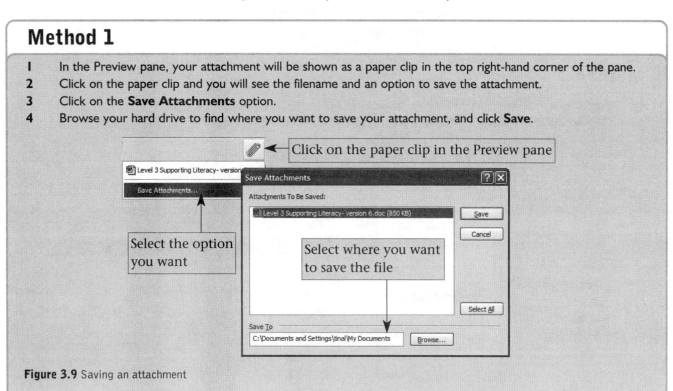

**Figure 3.9** Saving an attachment

## Method 2

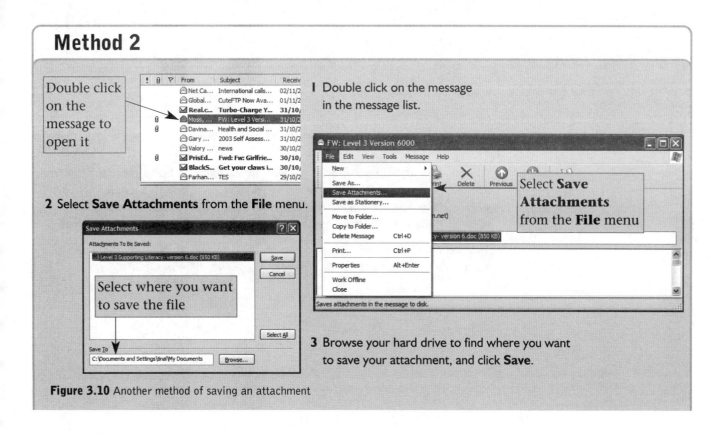

Double click on the message to open it

1 Double click on the message in the message list.

2 Select **Save Attachments** from the **File** menu.

Select where you want to save the file

Select **Save Attachments** from the **File** menu

3 Browse your hard drive to find where you want to save your attachment, and click **Save**.

**Figure 3.10** Another method of saving an attachment

Sometimes you may want to print out a copy of an e-mail message. Perhaps it contains information you need to complete a task, or instructions to go somewhere or do something.

## Method

1   Select the e-mail message you want to print.
2   Click on the **Print** button on the toolbar, or select **Print** from the **File** menu.
3   Check your printer settings.
4   Click on **OK**.

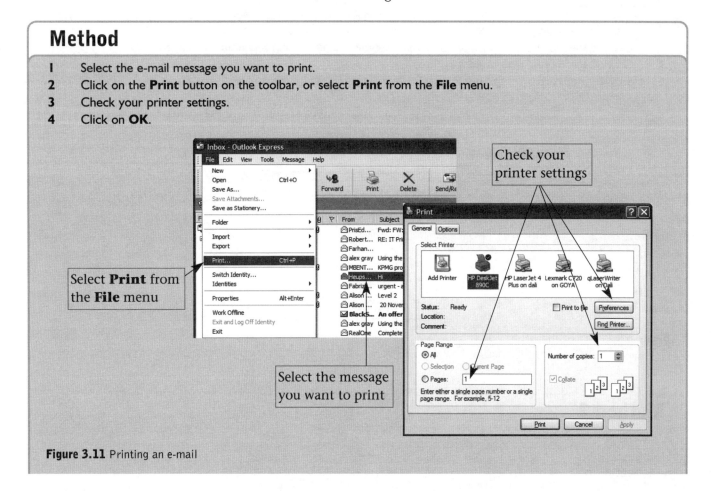

**Figure 3.11** Printing an e-mail

### Remember:

When you print out your e-mail, you will notice that it contains more information than you see in the Message pane when you open it. You will find information such as the e-mail address or name of the sender, your e-mail address (the recipient), the date and time the e-mail was sent, and the subject of the e-mail.

There is usually a header and a footer on the printout which show the date the e-mail was printed out and the number of pages in the messages.

## Task 3.7 | Printing e-mail attachments

### Method

1   Open your attachment. This could be either by double clicking the attachment in your e-mail message header or by opening it from its saved location using the appropriate program.
2   Use the **Print** option in the **File** menu of the program in which your attachment is then displayed.

## Task 3.8 | Deleting e-mails

If you're sending and receiving lots of e-mails, you'll soon find that your Inbox and Sent Items folders get rather full. When that happens it may be time to delete some of your old messages.

### Method

1   Select the e-mail message you want to delete.
2   Click on the **Delete** button on the toolbar, or select the **Delete** option in the **Edit** menu, or use the hotkey combination **Ctrl + D**.
3   The e-mail will be placed in your **Deleted Items** folder. You can open the folder to check it is there.

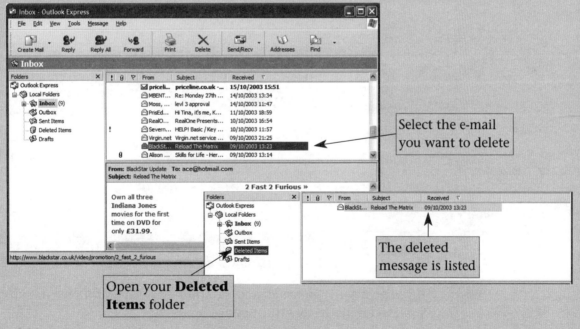

**Figure 3.12** Deleting an e-mail

You may decide that you don't want to keep any of your deleted messages in your Deleted Items folder when you close Outlook Express. You can do either of the following:

1   Select **Options** from the **Tools** menu.
2   Select the **Maintenance** tab.
3   Check the **Empty messages from the 'Deleted Items' folder on exit** box.

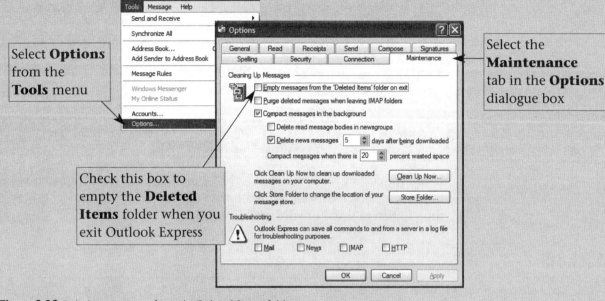

**Figure 3.13** Deleting messages from the Deleted Items folder

or

1   Select the **Empty 'Deleted Items' Folder** from the **Edit** menu on the toolbar.

**Figure 3.14** Another way of deleting messages from the Deleted Items folder

| Task 3.9 | Restoring a deleted e-mail message |
| --- | --- |

If you've deleted an e-mail and have not emptied your Deleted Items folder, you can always restore the message.

### Method

1   Open the Deleted Items folder.
2   Select the message to restore and hold down the mouse button.
3   Drag the message back to the Inbox or other folder.

## → Practise your skills 1

1 Open your e-mail program.

2 Check to see if you have any new mail. You should have a copy of the e-mail you sent in Practise your skills 4, Section 2.

3 Read your new mail.

4 Save the attachment to your hard drive.

5 Open the attachment from your e-mail program.

6 Print out a copy of the attachment.

7 Close your e-mail program.

Did you remember to virus check the attachment before you opened or saved it? Full marks if you did!

## → Practise your skills 2

1 Open your e-mail program.

2 Select the message you received from Practise your skills 4, Section 2.

3 Print out a copy of the message.

4 Delete the original message.

5 Close your e-mail program

## Task 3.10 | Forwarding an e-mail

One of the advantages of e-mails is that you can forward a message to someone else without having to type it out again. This can be very useful if you have received a message with some information that you need to share with someone else.

When you forward a message, the subject of the message will be entered in the **Subject** box automatically, but you can change it if you want to by highlighting and deleting the text and entering your own subject heading. You will need to enter the e-mail address of your recipient in the **To:** box.

## Method

| | |
|---|---|
| I | With the chosen message selected, click on the **Forward** button on the toolbar. |
| 2 | In the message window which opens, enter the e-mail address of the person to whom you want to forward the message. |
| 3 | If you want to add some text to the message, click in the message box and enter your text. |
| 4 | Send the message in the usual way. |

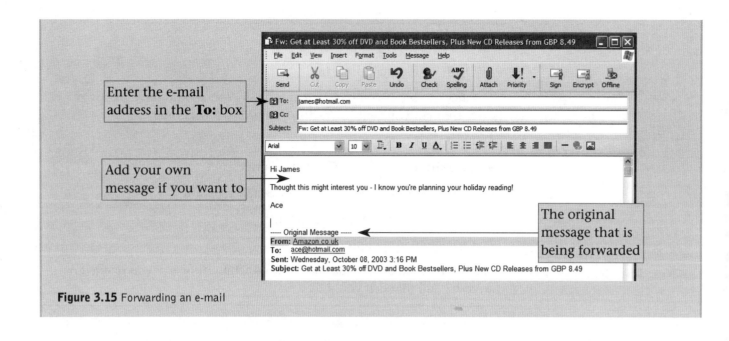

Enter the e-mail address in the **To:** box

Add your own message if you want to

The original message that is being forwarded

**Figure 3.15** Forwarding an e-mail

| Task 3.11 | Replying to e-mails |
| --- | --- |

Another advantage of e-mail is that you can reply to a message very easily. Using the **Reply** function, you can send back a copy of the message without having to type it again, or entering the recipient's address in the Address box. You can even use the same Subject heading unless you want to change it. You can add your own message to the text and your recipient will have a copy of the original message to refer to.

## Method

1   With the chosen message selected, click on the **Reply** button on the toolbar.
2   Click in the Message box and enter your text.
3   Send your message in the usual way.

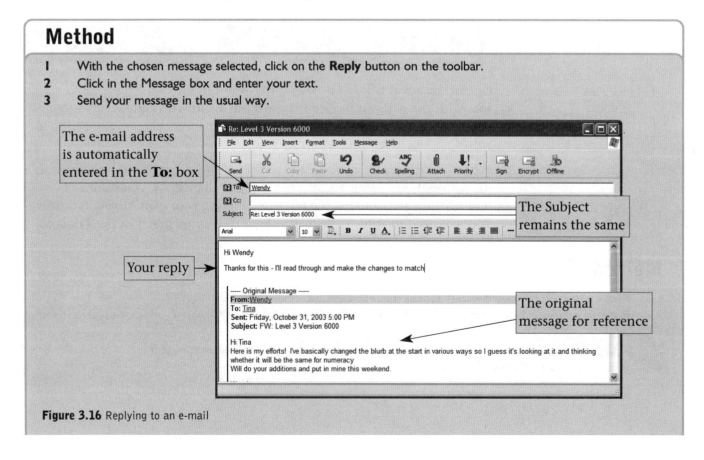

The e-mail address is automatically entered in the **To:** box

The Subject remains the same

Your reply

The original message for reference

**Figure 3.16** Replying to an e-mail

## Task 3.12 | Editing your messages

As mentioned previously, you can edit messages you have received before replying or forwarding them. This can be useful if you just want to use a part of the message in your reply, or if you want to add further information or answers to the message.

### Method

| | |
|---|---|
| 1 | Click on **Forward** or **Reply** to open the message window. |
| 2 | Highlight text you want to remove and use the **Cut** option in the **Edit** menu or the hotkeys **Ctrl + X**. |
| 3 | Place the cursor and click where you want to add extra text. Enter your text. |
| 4 | Insert text or other information from another file, document or e-mail message using the **Copy** and **Paste** functions, or the options from the **Insert** menu (see Section 2 for more information on inserting text and images into an e-mail message). |
| 5 | Send your message in the usual way. |

### Information

If you want to add text in a different colour, to show your replies for example, use the **Font Color** button **A** (note the American spelling of colour).

## Task 3.13 | Viewing message details

Being able to view the message details can give you a great deal of information about where your message has come from, how it reached you, when and by whom it was sent and, perhaps most importantly, the protocol used to send the message, such as MIME.

### Method

| | |
|---|---|
| 1 | Select **Properties** from the **File** menu. |
| 2 | Select the appropriate tab from the **Properties** dialogue box. |

| File Edit View Tools Message H |
|---|
| New ▶ |
| Open Ctrl+O |
| Save As... |
| Save Attachments... |
| Save as Stationery... |
| Folder ▶ |
| Import ▶ |
| Export ▶ |
| Print... Ctrl+P |
| Switch Identity... |
| Identities ▶ |
| Properties Alt+Enter |
| Work Offline |
| Exit and Log Off Identity |
| Exit |

**Figure 3.17** Properties

The **General** tab gives basic details about the message, such as:

- the size of the message in KB
- the subject and the sender
- the priority of the message
- the location of the message
- the dates sent and received

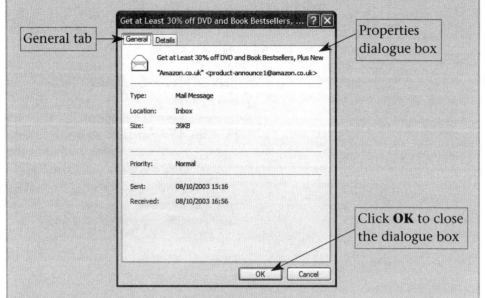

**Figure 3.18** General tab

The **Details** tab gives details such as:

- From
- To
- Subject
- Date
- Protocol used
- Content type

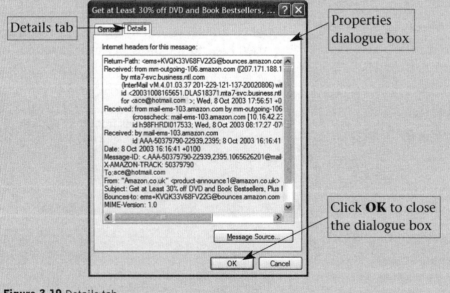

**Figure 3.19** Details tab

Hyperlinks can be inserted into e-mail messages which may link directly to download a file or program from a web page. Clicking on this link will take you to the web site and you can download the file onto your computer.

For example, you may have a link to a shareware program or to a file giving data, images or information. You will need to be connected to your ISP to access the web page.

## Information

When you download a file or program, you will need to remember that the larger the file, the longer it will take to download. The download time will also depend on the speed of your connection. Some web sites will tell you how big the file is before you start to download, which will give you an idea of how long it might take.

## Method

1  Click on the hyperlink in your e-mail message to take you to the web site.
2  Click on the **download** link on the web page (usually similar to a hyperlink or a button).
3  Select the **Save** option.
4  Choose where you want to save the file on your hard drive and click on **Save**.

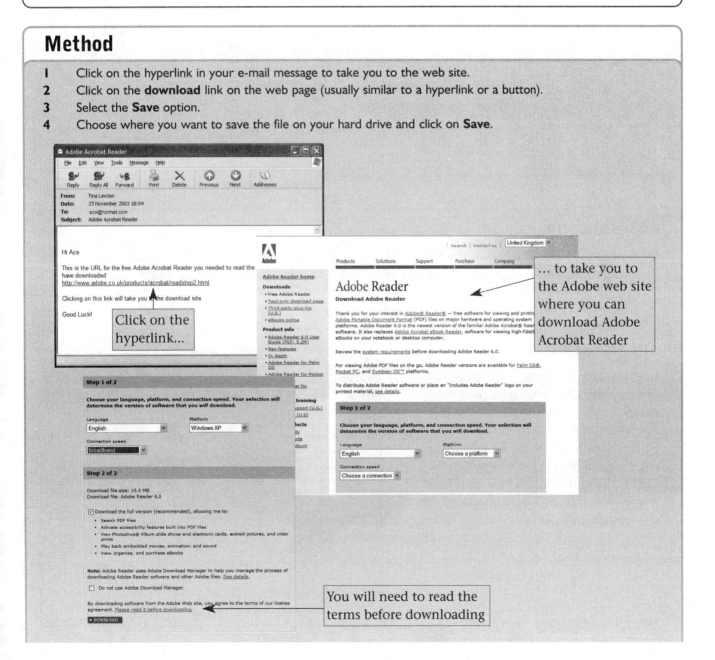

Click on the hyperlink...

... to take you to the Adobe web site where you can download Adobe Acrobat Reader

You will need to read the terms before downloading

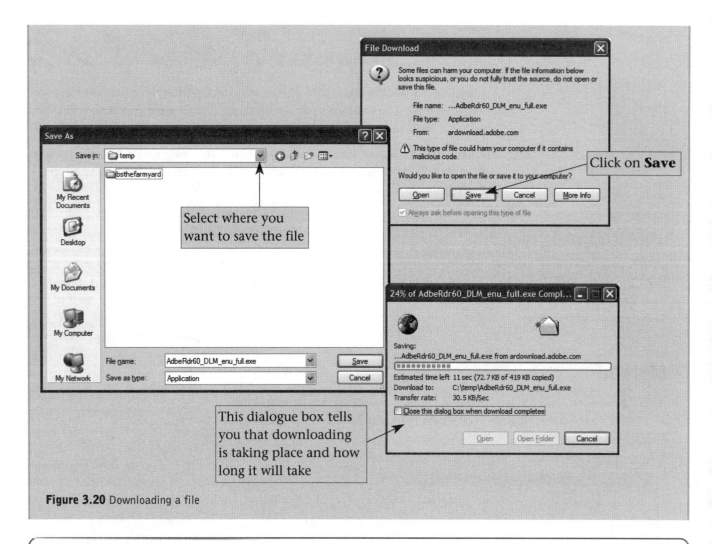

**Figure 3.20** Downloading a file

## Information

If you select **Open**, it will open the file to view or play straightaway (as long as you have the appropriate program loaded onto your computer). This will not download the program or file onto your hard drive.

## Information

In the example shown, the program is downloaded onto your hard drive (or wherever you have chosen to save it). You will still need to follow the instructions to open the file and set up the program before you can use it. This is the same process you would use if you were loading a new program from a floppy disk or CD-ROM.

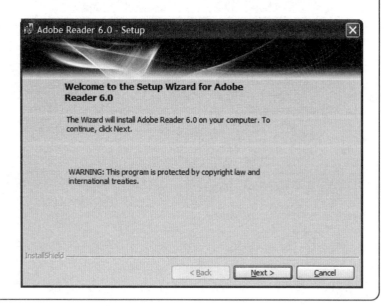

**Figure 3.21** Setting up a program

## Information

Because of the risk of viruses being transmitted from downloaded files, you should always use your virus checker to make sure the file is clear before you open it.

## Task 3.15 Blocking messages

You may find, for a variety of reasons, that you want to block e-mails from particular senders. Perhaps it is because you have received some junk e-mail from a business on the Net and don't want to keep having to spend time downloading their messages and deleting them from your Inbox, or maybe you have been receiving messages from someone you no longer want to correspond with. Whatever the reason, you can block the messages from senders such as these using a very simple option in your e-mail program.

## Method 1

1  Select the message from the sender you want to block.
2  Select **Block Sender** from the **Message** menu.
3  A prompt box will appear informing you that the sender has been added to your **blocked senders list.** Decide whether you want all current messages from this sender to be removed from the current folder by clicking on **Yes** or **No**.

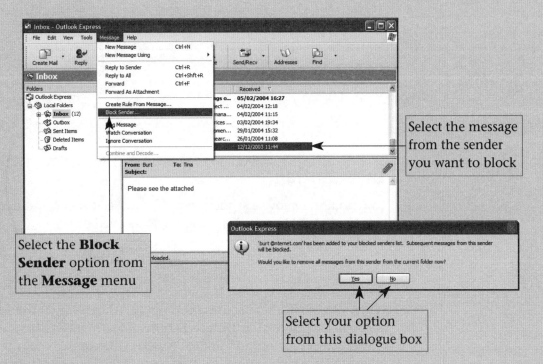

**Figure 3.22** Blocking a message

## Method 2

1  Select **Blocked Senders List** from the **Message Rules** option in the **Tools** menu.
2  Select the **Blocked Senders** tab in the **Message Rules** dialogue box.
3  Click on the **Add** button.
4  Enter the e-mail addresses of the sender you want to be blocked.
5  Click on **OK** to enter the e-mail address in the Blocked Senders List.
6  Click on **OK** to close the dialogue box.

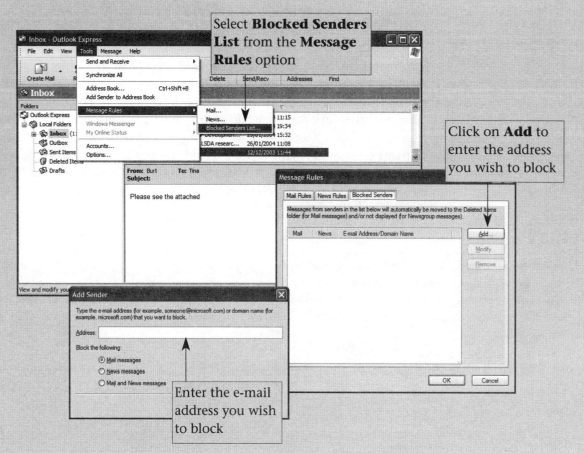

**Figure 3.23** Another method of blocking a message

## Information

You can also remove a sender from the Blocked Senders List by selecting the address and clicking the **Remove** button.

## Information

When you block a sender using this option, the messages will be diverted straight to your **Deleted Items** folder. You will have to remember to clear out this folder regularly otherwise it could get full of unwanted messages which will take up valuable space on your hard drive or network. Use the **Empty 'Deleted Items' Folder** option from the **Edit** menu, or check the **Empty messages from the 'Deleted Items' folder on exit** box in the **Options/Maintenance** settings. (See Task 3.8 on Page 57 for a quick revision!)

If you are away from your computer and wish to let the people who have sent e-mails know you are not at your computer, you can set up an automated reply to let them know you are not available.

## Method

1. Start a new mail message and enter the text you want to send back to people.
2. Save the file to your hard drive using the **Save As** function in the **File** menu.
3. Select the **Mail** option from the **Message Rules** option in the **Tools** menu.
4. In Section 1 of the **New Mail Rule** dialogue box, select the first condition for your rule. In this example it is the **Where the From line contains people** option.
5. In Section 3, select the underlined link <u>**contains people**</u>.
6. Enter the e-mail addresses of the people you want to include in the message rule and click **Add** after entering each address. When all addresses have been added, click on **OK**.
7. In Section 2, select the second condition for your rule. In this example it is the **Reply with message** option.
8. In Section 3, select the underlined link <u>**message**</u>.
9. Select the saved message file from the appropriate place on your hard drive.
10. Both your conditions will now be shown in the **New Message Rules** Section 3.
11. Click in the box in Section 4, and enter a name for your rule – in this case it is **Holiday**.
12. Click on **OK** and the **Message Rule** dialogue box shows that your rule is now operational. Click on **OK** to accept.

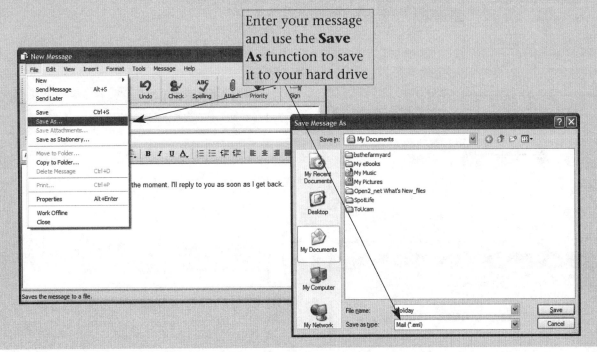

Enter your message and use the **Save As** function to save it to your hard drive

## Information

To send your automated reply, you will need to use the suggested file type **Mail (\*.eml)** in the **Save as type** drop down list box to save your message.

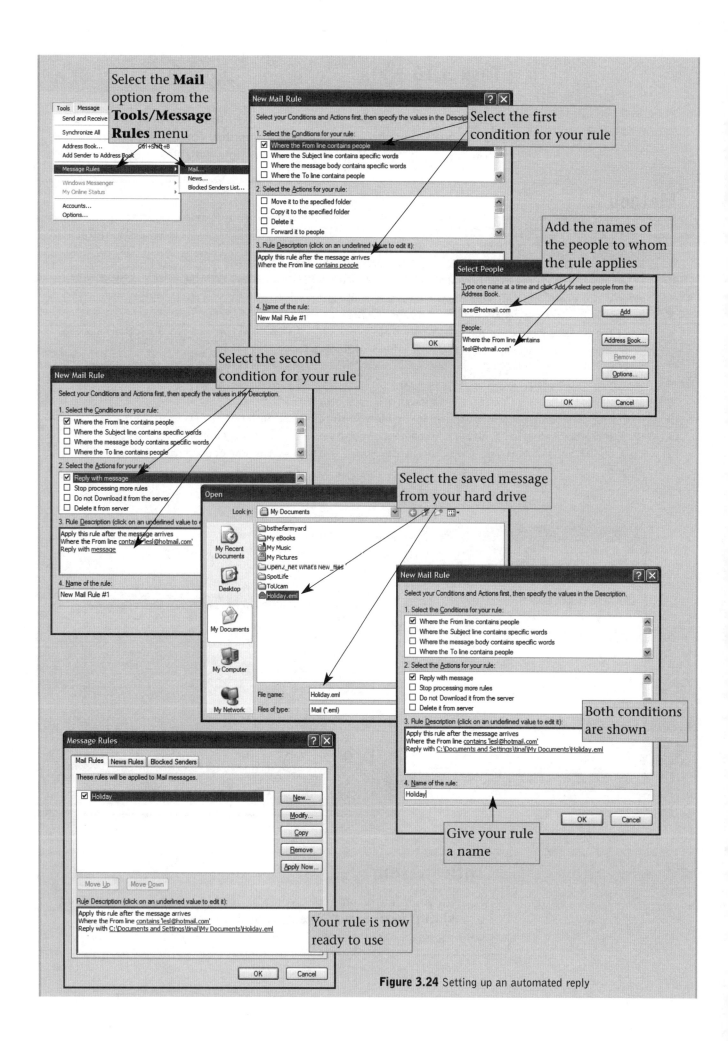

**Figure 3.24** Setting up an automated reply

<br>

## Hint:

To remove the rule, simply select it in the **Mail Rules/ Message Rules** dialogue box and click the **Remove** button.

## Information

You will need to be online to use this automated reply function. This would mean either leaving your computer switched on and connected to your ISP permanently, or setting it up to dial up your ISP at regular intervals. Both these options would mean your computer would have to be switched on all the time you were away. This might cause you some concern as many people wouldn't like to leave their machines on for such a period of time. The other consideration is the potential costs of either option, especially leaving your machine connected to your ISP for the whole period you were away. If you pay phone bills which vary with the amount of time spent online, it could get very expensive indeed, especially at peak rates.

## → Practise your skills 3

1 Open your e-mail program.
2 Check for new messages.
3 Select one of your messages, forward it to your tutor and send yourself a copy.
4 Select another message, reply to the sender and send a blind carbon copy to yourself.
5 Send your e-mails.
6 Close your e-mail program.

## → Practise your skills 4

1 Open your e-mail program.
2 Check for new messages.
3 Read the blind carbon copy of your message from the previous exercise and print out a copy.
4 Delete the message.
5 Close your e-mail program.

## → Practise your skills 5

1 Open your word processing program and enter the following text:

'There is always a danger when you download a file from the Internet or open an attachment to an e-mail message, that it could contain a virus. The only way to make sure you are safe from virus attack is to scan all downloaded files and attachments with a virus checker. To be any use, a virus checker should be updated regularly as new viruses are being produced all the time.

2 Save your file with the name **Beware of Viruses**.
3 Open your e-mail program and enter your own e-mail address in the Address box.
4 Enter a suitable word or phrase in the Subject box.

5 Attach your file **Beware of Viruses**.

6 Enter a suitable message in the message section.

7 Send the e-mail in the usual way.

8 Check to see if you've got new mail (hopefully your own file should be placed in your Inbox).

9 View the message properties and take a screen shot of the information. Print out a copy.

10 Save the attachment in a different location to the one you used before.

11 Open the attachment and print out a copy.

12 Close your e-mail program and disconnect.

Did you remember to virus check the attachment before you opened or saved it? Full marks if you did!

## → Practise your skills 6

1 Open your e-mail program.

2 Enter the e-mail address of someone you know or your tutor.

3 Enter an appropriate title in the Subject box.

4 Attach your file **Beware of Viruses**.

5 Enter a message in the message section, include the reason why you are sending the message and ask for an acknowledgement. Ask if they will send you an attachment in return.

6 Set the message as High Priority.

7 Send the e-mail in the usual way.

8 Close your e-mail program and disconnect.

## → Practise your skills 7

1 Open your e-mail program.

2 Check to see if you have any new mail.

3 If you receive a reply to your e-mail with an attachment, save the attachment to your hard drive.

4 Open the attachment and print out a copy.

5 Close your e-mail program and disconnect.

6 Open the program which is associated with the attachment you have received and load your saved file.

7 Print out a copy.

8 Close the program.

## → Practise your skills 8

1 Open your e-mail program.

2 Select the message you have received with your attachment from the above exercise and edit the message, using a coloured font to indicate your additions.

3 Forward the message to your tutor.

4 Close your e-mail program.

## → Practise your skills 9

1 Open your e-mail program.

2 Set up an automated reply to your tutor and yourself.

3 Ask your tutor to send you an e-mail.

4 Check with your tutor that the automated reply was sent. You could do this in another e-mail.

5 Remove the message rule which contains the automated reply.

6 Close your e-mail program.

## → Check your knowledge

1 How would you change the Layout view in your e-mail program?

2 How do you know if you have received new mail when you log on to your mail box at your ISP?

3 How can viruses be transmitted via e-mail?

4 How can you tell a new message has an attachment?

5 Why might you want to delete some e-mail messages?

6 What is the difference between replying to an e-mail and forwarding an e-mail?

7 What information can you find out from a mail message's properties?

8 What precautions should you take when downloading files?

9 How would you block a sender in your e-mail program? Why might you want to do this?

10 What problems could you see in using the automated reply function in your e-mail program?

## You will learn to

- Explain that messages can become unmanageable if not sorted
- Create folders to store e-mail messages
- Move or copy messages to other folders
- Add, delete or switch folders
- Retrieve e-mails from an e-mail filing system
- Describe systematic storage of messages
- Describe the management of e-mails from several accounts
- Store messages on a mail server and describe the issues of storing too many e-mails

## Managing your folders

Just as you sometimes need to sort out your paper correspondence, so you might need to tidy up and organise your e-mail folders. This can be a helpful way to get your mail sorted into different categories, such as: mail from friends, from work, or from family. In the previous Section you will have found out that deleting e-mails you no longer want can help to keep your folders tidy. You can also use some of the maintenance functions to compact your messages or even hide them if you don't want to delete them.

Saving all your e-mails, especially if you share your computer with your family, can take up quite a large chunk of your disk space, so being aware of good housekeeping can be important.

## Task 4.1 — Creating a new folder

Creating folders to store your messages is a very handy way of organising your Inbox. Imagine that you regularly receive e-mails from work and from friends and you want to keep them in separate folders. By creating a folder for work e-mails and another for your friends, you can keep your messages tidy. If you need to find an e-mail message from a work colleague, you will only need to look in your work folder rather than having to scroll through all the messages you have ever received.

## Method

| | |
|---|---|
| 1 | Use the right mouse button to click on one of the folders in the Folders list. |
| 2 | Select **New Folder** from the pop-up menu. |
| 3 | Enter the name you wish to give to the new folder in the **Folder name:** box. |
| 4 | Select the folder you wish to create the new folder in. |
| 5 | Click on **OK**. |

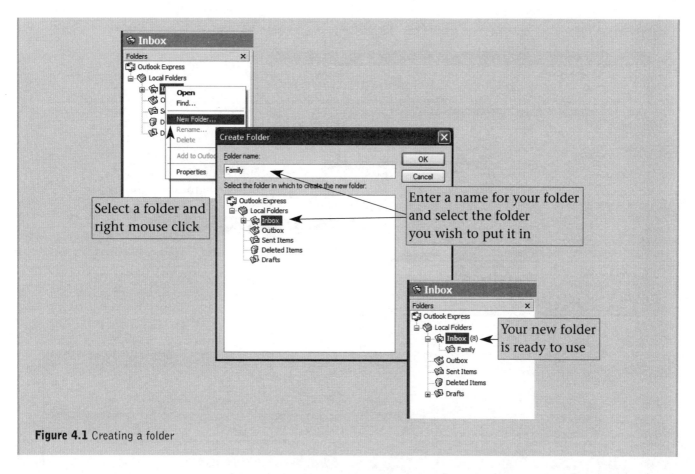

**Figure 4.1** Creating a folder

If you now open your selected folder, you should see your new folder in the list.

## Information

You can **add** new folders to your local folders list whenever you need extra folders to sort and store your e-mails. You can also add folders within any other folder to subdivide your e-mail storage system.

| Task 4.2 | Moving messages into a folder |

Having created a new folder, you can now move messages into it.

## Method

| | |
|---|---|
| 1 | Right mouse click on the message you wish to move. |
| 2 | Select **Move to Folder** from the pop-up menu. |
| 3 | Select the folder you want to move the message to. |
| 4 | Click on **OK**. |

If you open the folder, your message should now be shown in the message list.

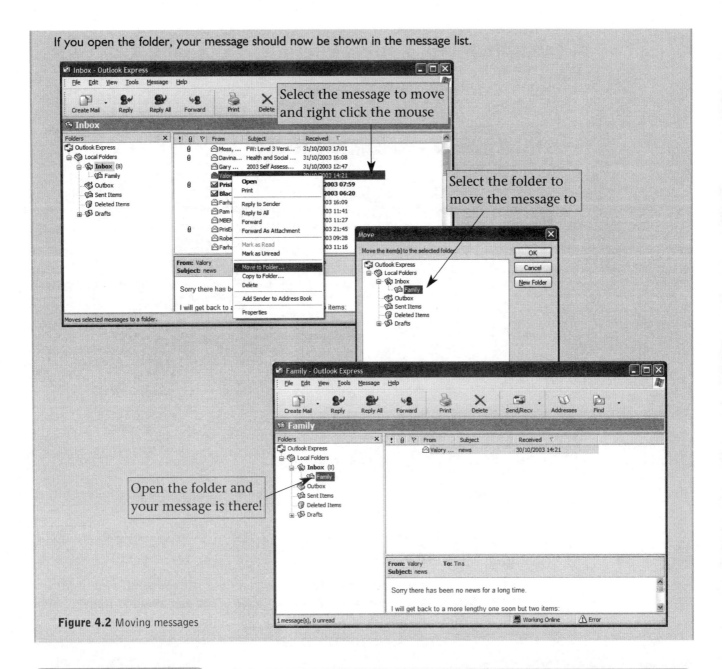

**Figure 4.2** Moving messages

**Hint:**

You can also copy a message to another folder using the method in Task 4.2, by choosing the **Copy to Folder** option.

**Hint:**

If you have both the message list and the folder list in view, you can also click on the message, hold down the mouse button and drag the message to the appropriate folder.

| Task 4.3 | Deleting folders |
|---|---|

Sometimes you might find that you no longer use a folder and want to delete it to tidy up your Inbox.

## Method

| | |
|---|---|
| 1 | Select the folder you want to delete. |
| 2 | Select the **Delete** option in the **File/Folder** menu on the toolbar. |
| 3 | Confirm that you want to delete the folder by clicking on **Yes** in the warning box which appears. |

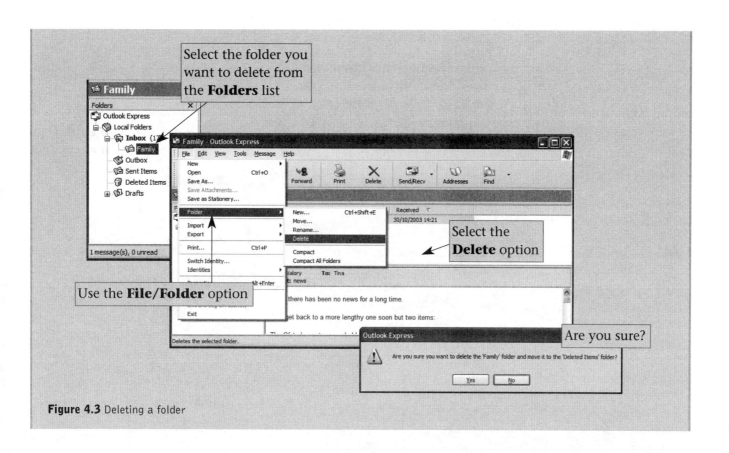

Select the folder you want to delete from the **Folders** list

Select the **Delete** option

Use the **File/Folder** option

Are you sure?

**Figure 4.3** Deleting a folder

## Task 4.4 | Switching folders

Having created new folders, and sorted out your e-mails, you need to switch between your folders to access your messages.

### Method

| | |
|---|---|
| 1 | With your folders list in view, select the folder you want to open. |
| 2 | To open another folder, click on the folder in the folders list. |

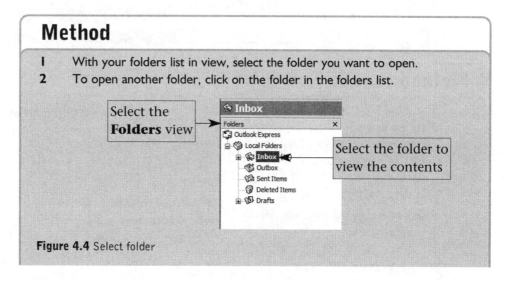

Select the **Folders** view

Select the folder to view the contents

**Figure 4.4** Select folder

or

1　Select **Go to Folder** from the **View** menu.

2　Select the folder you want to open from the list.

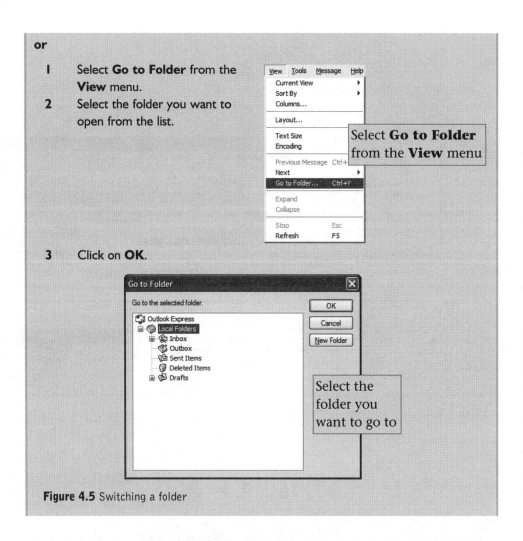

Select **Go to Folder** from the **View** menu

3　Click on **OK**.

Select the folder you want to go to

**Figure 4.5** Switching a folder

## Task 4.5　Retrieving e-mail messages from folders

## Method

1　Select the folder where the message is stored to open it and view all the messages in the message list.

2　Select the message to view it.

or

1　Select **Message** from the **Find** option in the **Edit** menu.

2　Accept the folder name in the **Look in** field or **Browse** and select the folder from the list which appears.

3　Enter any details you can remember in the appropriate boxes, such as From, To, Subject or Message.

4　Click on the **Find Now** button.

5　Select the message you want from the list which appears below.

6　Double click on the message in the list to open it, or select **Open** from the **File** menu.

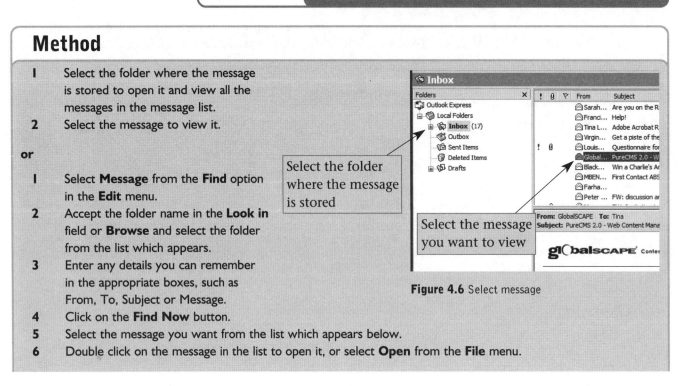

Select the folder where the message is stored

Select the message you want to view

**Figure 4.6** Select message

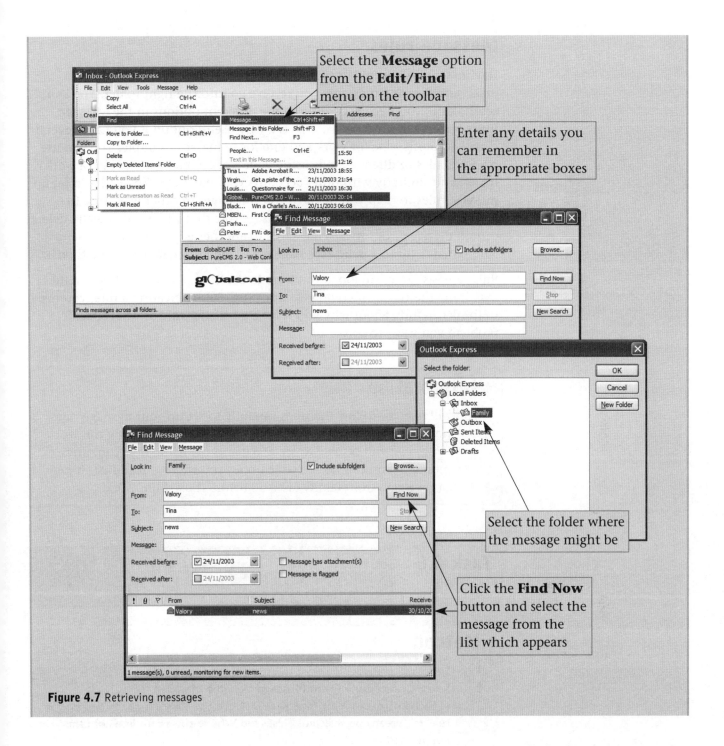

**Figure 4.7** Retrieving messages

## Information

Using the **Find** option is very useful once you start to send and receive e-mails. It can be surprising how quickly your folders can fill up with messages if you use your e-mail program often. Once you start having to click on folders and scrolling through your messages, it can take quite some time before you find the one you need – especially if you have several subfolders for different messages and use the **Message Rules** options to direct your e-mails to other folders, as shown in the following Tasks.

## Message rules

Having set up your folders, you can use the Message Rules functions to make sure that any messages you receive go into the right folder. You can set the rules you need according to the different options in the Message Rules box to suit your needs. This is a very useful option if you have several e-mail accounts, one for work and one for home, for example. You can use message rules to direct e-mails using your work e-mail address into a work folder, and similarly with other accounts you may have. You can also set up message rules to help you manage your messages in other ways too. In Outlook Express you can set up a message rule that will automatically delete certain messages, or forward messages to another e-mail address, or send an automated reply to e-mails (see page 67, Using automated reply methods).

Rules are easy to create once you have had a little practice, but be careful of overdoing the rules – it could get confusing. Before creating a rule, you need to think carefully about why you want a particular rule or what specific problem you want to solve.

### Information

You will need to follow the steps carefully to set up your message rules, but the time spent doing this will make life easier in the long run. For one thing, you will be able to see at a glance which folders contain new messages and can decide which ones you want to read first. It may be that messages from family are read before those from work!

| Task 4.6 | Creating message rules from a message |
|----------|----------------------------------------|

### Method

<div class="hint">

**Hint:**

You can use the message rules to set various other options for your messages. This example shows the method for setting a message rule to sort messages into different folders.

</div>

1  Select the message you want to use to create a rule.
2  Select **Create Rule From Message** from the **Message** menu.
3  In Section 1 of the **New Mail Rule** dialogue box, the first condition for your rule will already be selected. This is the **Where the From line contains people** option.
4  In Section 3, the **rule description** has already been entered showing the e-mail address of the contact.
5  In Section 2, select the **Move it to the specified folder** option by checking the box.
6  In Section 3, click on the underlined link **specified**, and select the folder from the folders list which appears.
7  Click in the box in Section 4 and enter a name for your rule.
8  Click on **OK** and the **Message Rule** dialogue box shows that your rule is now operational. Click on **OK** to accept.

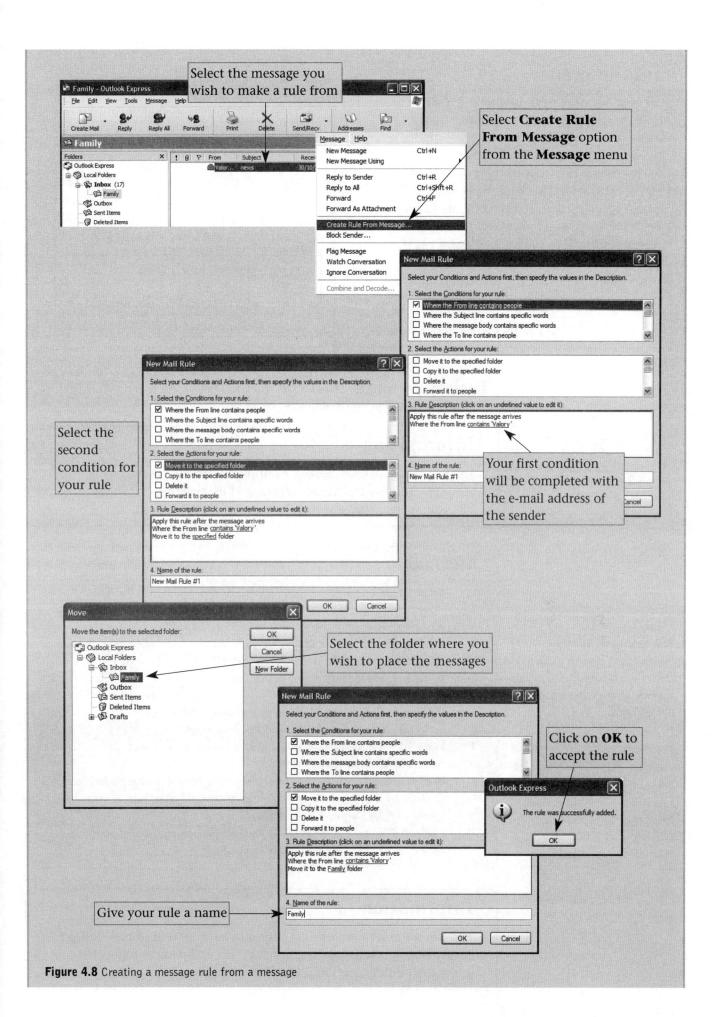

**Figure 4.8** Creating a message rule from a message

## Information

All your message rules are listed in the upper section of the Message Rules dialogue box. Outlook Express only applies rules when the boxes are checked. This makes it very easy to turn rules off and on by checking or unchecking the boxes. When you click on a rule's name, its description appears in the Rule Description section of the dialogue box. You can change any of the details in the rule description, or rewrite the rule completely by clicking the **Modify** button.

**Figure 4.9** Message Rules dialogue box

## Task 4.7 — Creating message rules for e-mails

### Information

The following method uses an example of setting a message rule to sort messages from several accounts, but you may want to set other rules to suit your own message storage and management system.

### Hint:

You could use message rules to sort your e-mails from a web-based account, such as Hotmail, and your ISP account.

### Hint:

To remove a rule, simply select it in the **Mail Rules/ Message Rules** dialogue box and click the **Remove** button.

### Method

1. Select the **Mail** option from the **Message Rules** option in the **Tools** menu.
2. In Section 1 of the **New Mail Rule** dialogue box, select the first condition for your rule. If you are creating a rule to sort messages from different accounts, you would check the **Where the message is from the specified account** box.
3. In Section 3, select the underline link **specified**.
4. In the **Select Account** dialogue box, select the account you want to use for this rule. Click on **OK**.
5. In Section 2, check the **Move it to the specified folder** box.
6. In Section 3, select the underlined link **specified**.
7. In the **Move** dialogue box, select the folder where you want the messages to be placed. Click on **OK**.
8. Both your conditions will now be shown in the **New Message Rules** Section 3.
9. Click in the box in Section 4 and enter a name for your rule – it may be something like **Family**, for example.
10. Click on **OK** and the **Message Rule** dialogue box shows that your rule is now operational. Click on **OK** to accept.

### Information

You can set more than one condition in each section of the Message Rule dialogue box. For each condition you will need to follow the underlined link in Section 3 to define the rule.

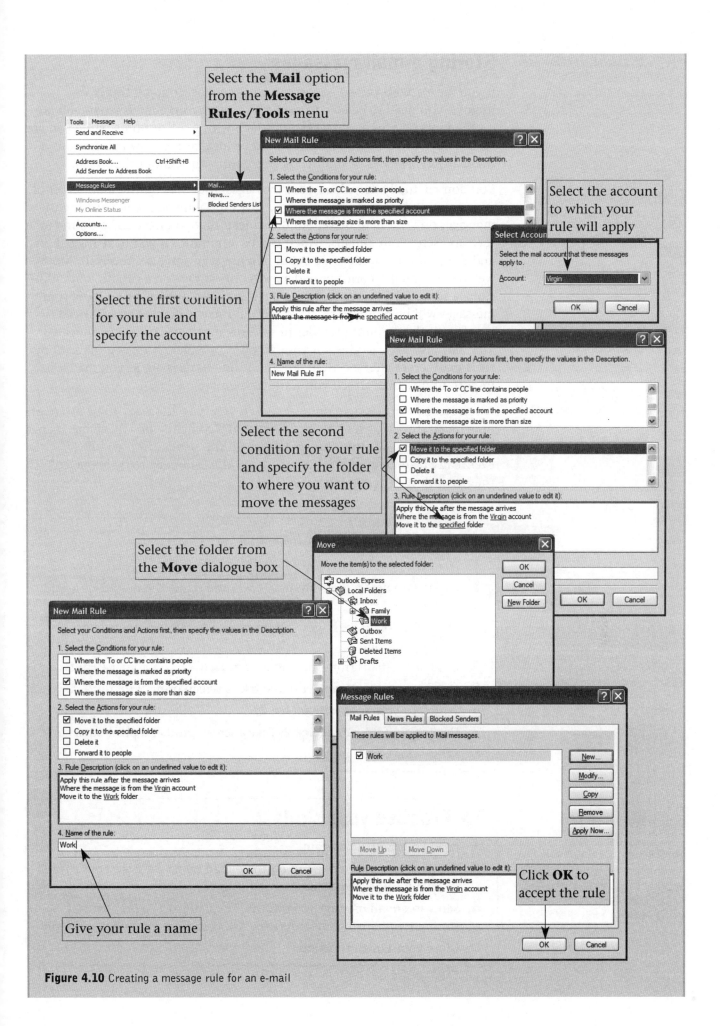

Select the **Mail** option from the **Message Rules/Tools** menu

Select the account to which your rule will apply

Select the first condition for your rule and specify the account

Select the second condition for your rule and specify the folder to where you want to move the messages

Select the folder from the **Move** dialogue box

Give your rule a name

Click **OK** to accept the rule

**Figure 4.10** Creating a message rule for an e-mail

# Storing e-mail messages

If you have a **web-based** e-mail account, such as Hotmail, this is very useful if you need to be able to read and answer your e-mails when you are on the move. If you need to keep in touch with work or home while you are on holiday, a web-based account would be ideal as it can be accessed from the many cyber cafés or Internet access points throughout the world.

You don't actually download your messages; they stay on the mail server of your account provider. This certainly saves space if you are not storing the messages on your hard drive, but does mean that you have to be online to read and send your e-mails, which can be a nuisance if you have logged off and then want to check some detail in a message you have received. Most web-based e-mail account providers will only allow you a certain amount of storage space for your messages, and when that space has been filled, some messages will be removed to make space for new e-mails. You will need to check with the account provider to see how much space you are allocated. You may also need to check if your account provider removes e-mails from their mail server after a certain length of time has passed, as you may lose important messages which you want to keep.

If you store your messages on a **network** you may also need to be aware of how much storage space you are allowed. If a company or college has many e-mail users who all store their messages on the server, they would eventually take up quite a lot of space and this will need to be managed by the network system administrator.

## → Practise your skills 1

1 Load your e-mail program.
2 Create two new folders in your Inbox and name them Practice 1 and Practice 2.
3 Move the e-mail messages you have already received throughout this unit to your new folder **Practice 1**.
4 Copy the e-mails from the folder **Practice 1** to the folder **Practice 2**.
5 Open your folder **Practice 1** and take a screen print. Print out a copy.
6 Switch to your folder **Practice 2.**
7 Delete your folder **Practice 2**. Take a screen print and print out a copy.
8 Close your e-mail program.

## → Practise your skills 2

1 Load your e-mail program.
2 Create a message rule to put all the e-mail messages from your tutor into your folder **Practice 1**.
3 Send an e-mail message to your tutor explaining the problems of storing too many e-mail messages. Ask your tutor to send you a reply.
4 Close your e-mail program.

## → Practise your skills 3

1 Load your e-mail program.

2 Check for new mail.

3 Go to your folder **Practice 1** and check for new messages. Hopefully your tutor will have replied.

4 Read the message and print out a copy.

5 Close your e-mail program.

## → Practise your skills 4

1 Load your e-mail program.

2 Retrieve the message from your tutor and send a reply to acknowledge that you have received it.

3 Close your e-mail program.

# Consolidation 2

1 Select an image, which could be clip art or a photo, which you have on your computer. Open your word processing program and enter some text describing the image. Save your file to an appropriate place with the filename **Image description**.

2 Open your e-mail program, start a new message and enter your own address in the To: box and your tutor's e-mail address in the Cc: box.

3 Enter a suitable word or phrase in the Subject box.

4 Attach your file **Image description**.

5 Enter the following text in Arial font, size 12:

'A description of the image shown below can be accessed from the attached file.'

6 Insert the image into your e-mail.

7 Create a suitable signature and add this to your e-mail message.

8 Send the e-mail in the usual way and disconnect from your ISP.

9 Create a folder in your Inbox with the name **Copy Messages**.

10 Create a message rule to sort all your own copy messages into the new folder you have created.

11 Connect to your ISP and check for new mail (hopefully your own message will be received).

12 Save the attachment to a different location from the one you used before.

13 Save the e-mail to an appropriate place.

14 Disconnect from your ISP.

15 Locate the saved files and open them in the appropriate programs. Print out copies of both files.

16 Delete the **Copy Messages** folder from your Inbox and the rule you created from the message rules.

17 Close your e-mail program.

# Section 5 Using an address book

## You will learn to

- Access an address book
- Add addresses
- Delete and edit addresses
- Identify the use of e-mail aliases
- Create e-mail groups or aliases in an address book
- Describe how to organise an address book
- Search an address book to retrieve the addresses or group of addresses for e-mails
- Identify when an address book would be used

## Address book

Just as your paper-based address book holds information about family, friends and other contacts, so your e-mail program offers a similar electronic facility. The main difference is that you don't need to write the details by hand, or have lots of crossings out as addresses change over time – it's much easier with your electronic version!

Most address book facilities in e-mail programs allow you to enter more details than just the bare name and e-mail address. You will find that you can also enter other useful information, including home addresses and phone numbers, business details, and even important dates such as birthdays and anniversaries.

## Task 5.1 Accessing the Address Book

### Method

1 Open your e-mail program.

2 Click on the **Addresses** button on the toolbar 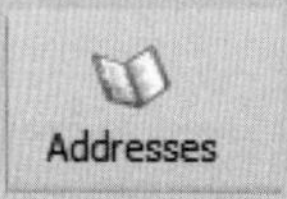

, or select the **Address Book** from the **Tools** menu.

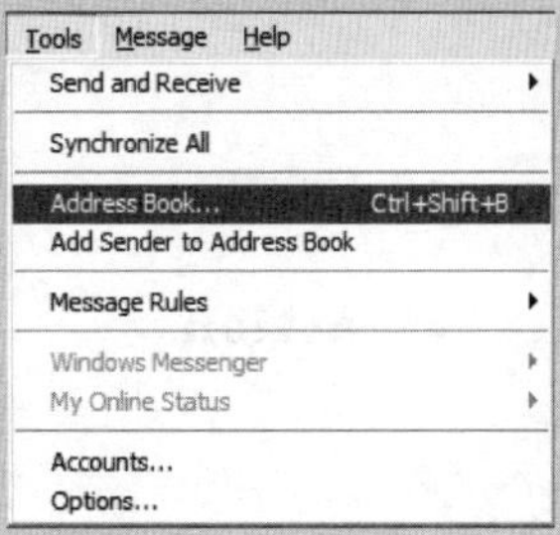


**Figure 5.1** Address book

**3** The **Address Book** will open.

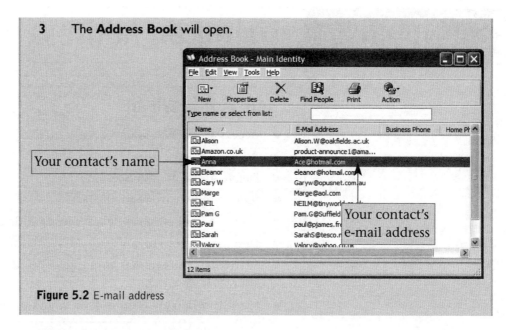

**Figure 5.2** E-mail address

## Address Book toolbar

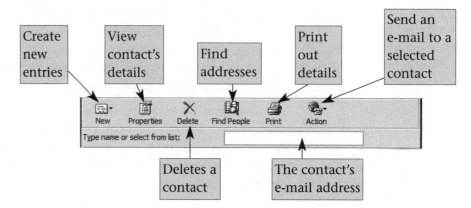

**Figure 5.3** Address Book toolbar

- **New**          This option allows you to create a new entry in your address book.
- **Properties**   You can view the details of each contact in your address book.
- **Delete**       When you no longer want to keep an address in your address book you can use this option to delete the details.
- **Find People**  Use this option to search for specific people in your address book. This can be very useful if you find that you've got a large number of addresses and scrolling through them all gets time-consuming.
- **Print**        This option allows you to print information about the selected contact or contacts.
- **Action**       Amongst other options, you can choose to send mail to the selected contact.

## Task 5.2    Adding addresses

## Method 1 From a selected message

**Either**

I    Right click the mouse on the message in the message list and select **Add Sender to Address Book** from the pop-up menu.

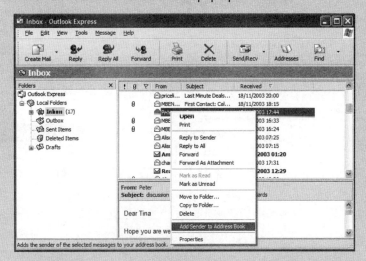

**Figure 5.4** Adding an address automatically

2    The address is added automatically to your address book.

**or**

I    With the message selected, choose **Add Sender to Address Book** from the **Tools** menu.

2    The address is added automatically to your address book.

**Figure 5.5** Another way of adding to your address book

## Method 2 Entering an address manually

I    Open the address book.

2    Select **New Contact** from the **File** menu or select the drop down menu from the **New** button on the toolbar.

3    In the **Properties** box, enter the details of your new contact, including their name, nickname and e-mail address, in the boxes under the **Name** tab.

4    Click on the **Add** button to add the e-mail address to your address book.

5    Enter any other details you want to record under the other tabs available, such as birthday, business address, etc.

6    Click on **OK** to close the Properties box.

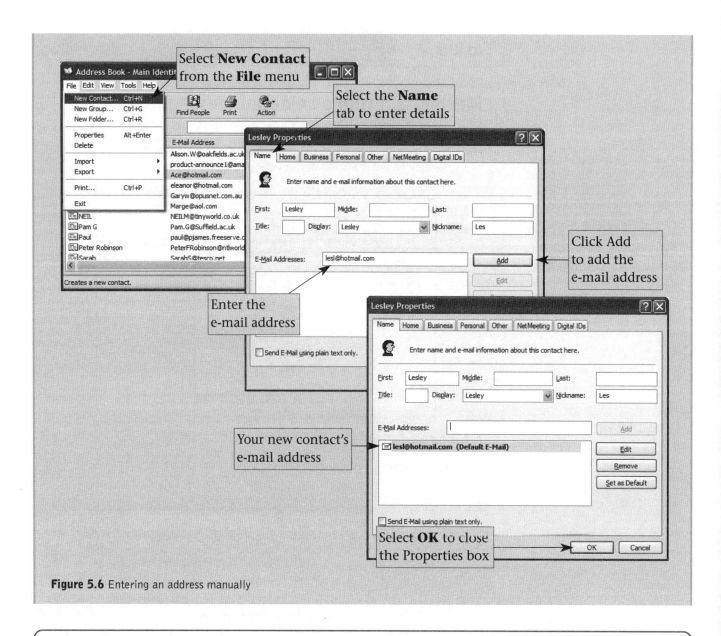

**Figure 5.6** Entering an address manually

## Information

Instead of the whole e-mail address or the name appearing in the **contact list**, you can give your contact an e-mail nickname and select this to be displayed. Enter the nickname in the appropriate field in the contact's Properties box, and select the name you want to use from the drop down list box in the **Display** field.

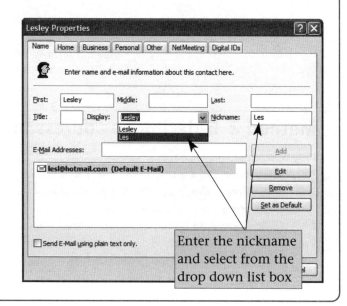

**Figure 5.7** Entering a nickname

## Task 5.3    Deleting addresses

You may find over time that some of the contact details may no longer be valid. Perhaps they have new e-mail addresses, or perhaps you no longer send messages to them. Whatever the reason, you will have addresses that you no longer want, which you can delete to make your address book less cluttered.

## Method

1    Open your address book.
2    Select the contact you want to delete.
3    Select **Delete** from the **File** menu, or press the **Delete** key on your keyboard.
4    Click on **OK** in the warning box which appears (just as long as you are sure you want to delete the contact details!).
5    Check that the contact details have been deleted from the address book and close it.

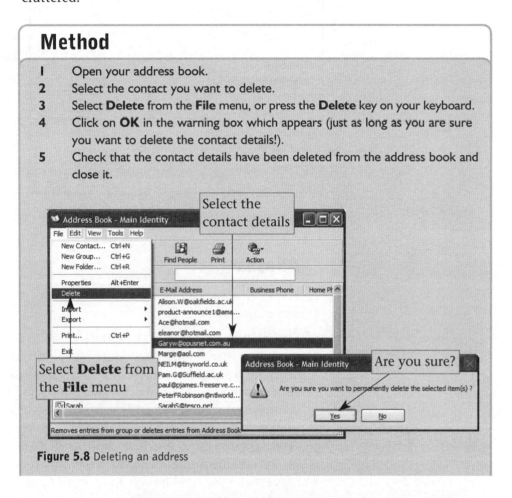

**Figure 5.8** Deleting an address

## Task 5.4    Editing addresses

Sometimes you may need to change or edit an address in your address book; if you had the address slightly wrong, for example, and correcting it would be easier than re-entering it all.

## Method

1    Open your address book.
2    Select the contact you want to edit.
3    Select **Properties** from the **File** menu, or click the **Properties** button

      on the toolbar.
Properties

4    Select the **Name** tab, and click the **Edit** button.

**5**      Edit the address.

**6**      Click on **OK** to implement the change.

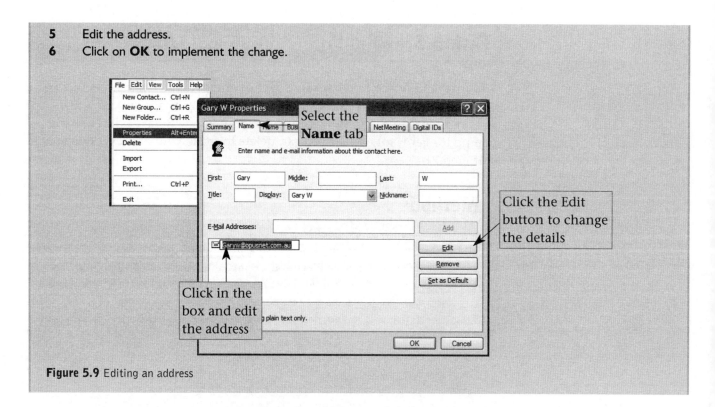

**Figure 5.9** Editing an address

## Aliases

The word **alias** can be used in two different contexts when sending and receiving e-mails.

Many ISPs offer a number of different e-mail addresses which all come through a shared e-mail account and are referred to as **aliases**. This would be useful if several members of a family used the same e-mail account, as each member could have their own e-mail address, or alias. For example, if you have a Freeserve account you could have e-mail addresses such as *Joe@cheznous.freeserve.co.uk*, *Sarah@cheznous.freeserve.co.uk* and *Work@cheznous.freeserve.co.uk*, which will all use the same mailbox facility. To sort the incoming messages you would need to set up folders for each address and use the Message Rules options as shown in Section 4, to make sure that everyone's e-mails ended up in their own Inbox.

**Alias** is also used for the name given to a group of contacts in an address book. If you find that you often send the same e-mail to a group of people you can create a single group to use instead, you can then select the group name or alias from the contact's list, which is much quicker than having to use all the individual addresses. It may also mean that you don't leave someone out of the correspondence by accident – it might cause offence if you did!

## Method

1    Open your address book.
2    Select **New Group** from the drop down menu of the **New** button, or from the **File** menu.
3    In the **Group Properties** box enter the Group Name.
4    Click on the **Select Members** button to open the list of contacts in the address book.
5    Select each contact you want to add to your group and click the **Select** button to add the details to the right-hand pane.
6    Click on **OK** to enter the names in your group in the Group Properties box.
7    Click on **OK** to return to your address book. The new group is shown in the list of contacts in bold type.

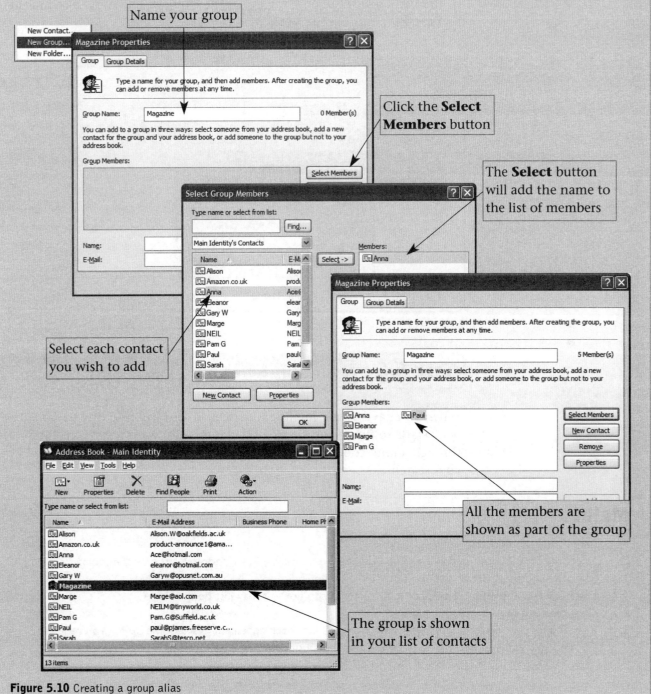

**Figure 5.10** Creating a group alias

## Information

You can **add** contact details manually by entering the name and e-mail address in the Group Properties box. Simply click the **Add** button to add the contact to your group.

To **delete** a contact, select the name and click the **Remove** button.

## Information: Organising an address book

There are several ways to organise your address book to help you find a contact or groups more easily. You can sort them alphabetically by first or last name, by e-mail address, or by phone number by clicking on the particular heading at the top of the column. You could also use the **Sort By** option in the **View** menu.

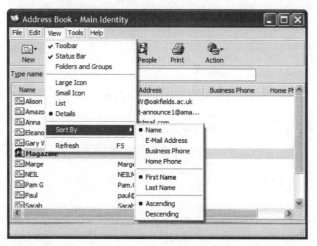

**Figure 5.11** Organising an address book

## Task 5.6 | Finding an address

When you have been e-mailing for a while, you may find that your address book starts to fill up and finding the address you want means scrolling through a long contact list. You can use the **Find** option to help speed up your search.

## Method

| | |
|---|---|
| 1 | Open your address book. |
| 2 | Select the **Find People** option from the **Edit** menu or click the **Find People** button on the toolbar. |
| 3 | Select the **Address Book** from the **Look in:** drop down list box. |
| 4 | Enter any details you can remember in the appropriate box – it may just be the name. |
| 5 | Click the **Find Now** button. |
| 6 | Right mouse click on the address you want from the list which appears and select the option you require. |
| | To send an e-mail to the contact, select the **Send Mail** option. |

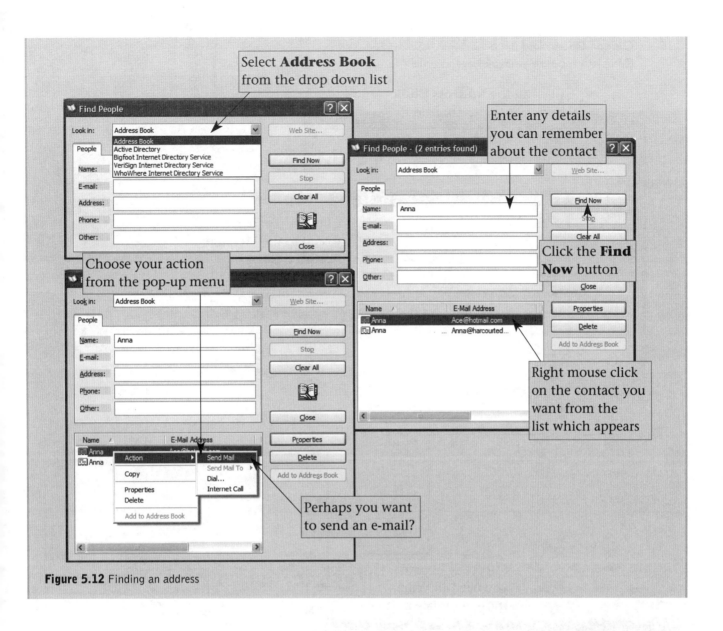

**Figure 5.12** Finding an address

Labels within the figure:

Select **Address Book** from the drop down list

Enter any details you can remember about the contact

Click the **Find Now** button

Right mouse click on the contact you want from the list which appears

Choose your action from the pop-up menu

Perhaps you want to send an e-mail?

---

| Task 5.7 | **Using an address book** |

Using an address book can save a great deal of time and effort when sending e-mails. It can be very difficult to remember all the e-mail addresses of the people you e-mail often, let alone the people you only contact occasionally. This is where the address book comes into its own, and, because it is so useful, it is well worth keeping it up to date.

## Method

1. Start a new mail message.
2. Click on the **Address Book** icon 📖 To: next to the **To:** box.
3. Select the contact from the address book list.
4. Click the **To:** button  To: ->  to add the contact to the **To:** box, or click the **Cc:** button  Cc: -> , or the

   **Bcc:** button  Bcc: ->  to add a contact to either of these fields.
5. Repeat this with all the contacts you want to include in the e-mail – this might include your group as well.

**6**   Click on **OK** to close the box.

**7**   Complete and send your message as usual.

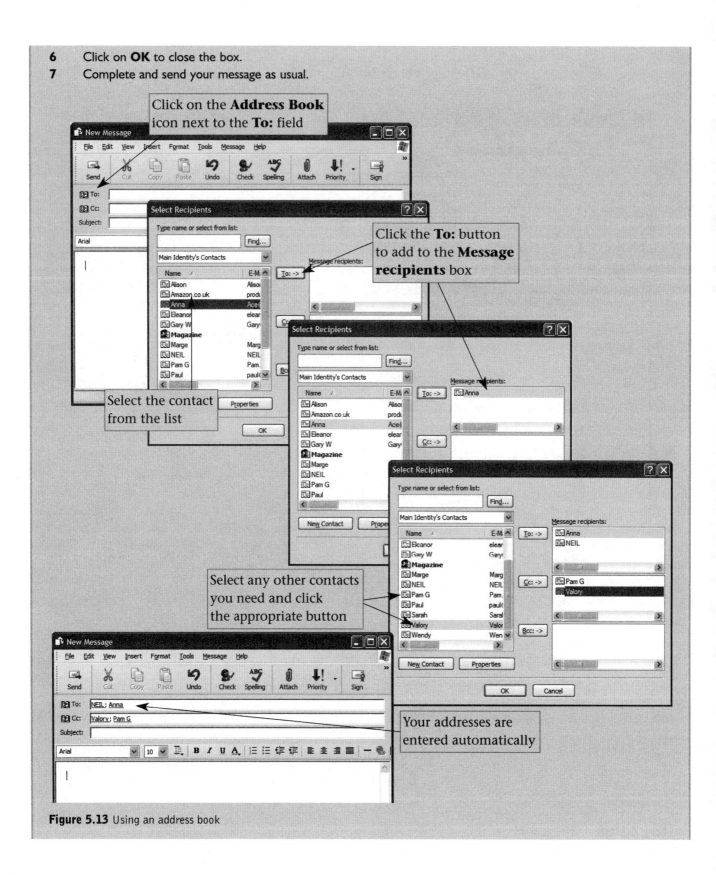

Click on the **Address Book** icon next to the **To:** field

Click the **To:** button to add to the **Message recipients** box

Select the contact from the list

Select any other contacts you need and click the appropriate button

Your addresses are entered automatically

**Figure 5.13** Using an address book

## → Practise your skills 1

1 Load your e-mail program.

2 Open your address book and check to see if your tutor's e-mail address is shown. Delete it if so.

3 Using one of the messages from your tutor, enter the e-mail address details in your address book.

4 Enter the following e-mail address details in your address book:

Josie Bennett, josie@heinemann.co.uk, Nickname: JosieB.
Ali Muhammed, alim@supersurfer.co.uk, Nickname: Ali

5 Create a group with the alias **Practice** in your address book for your tutor, Josie and Ali.

6 Compose an e-mail message to the group explaining that you have created a group contact list.

7 Save the message in your **Drafts** folder (**Don't send it – the two addresses you have just added are fictitious!**)

8 Open your Drafts folder, take a screen print and print a copy.

9 Close your e-mail program.

## → Practise your skills 2

1 Load your e-mail program.

2 Delete the message in your Drafts folder.

3 Ali has changed his e-mail address, it should now be:
ali@hotmail.com.
Edit the details in your address book to show the new address.

4 Take a screen print of your address book and print out a copy.

5 Close your e-mail program.

## → Practise your skills 3

1 Load your e-mail program.

2 Delete the group contact details in your address book.

3 Delete the e-mail addresses for Ali and Josie from your address book.

4 Close your e-mail program.

## → Practise your skills 4

1 Load your e-mail program.

2 Start a new e-mail message to your tutor using the address book facility to enter the address in the **To:** box.

3 Compose a message about using the **Find** option to locate an e-mail address in your address book.

4 Send your message and close your e-mail program.

## → Check your knowledge

1   Why would you use an address book facility in an e-mail program?

2   Label the toolbar diagram with the functions shown by the arrows:

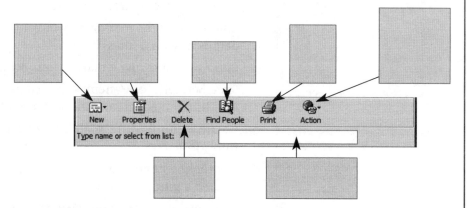

3   What benefits would there be in creating a contact group or alias in your address book?

4   How would you use the address book in your e-mail program?

# Practice assignments

## Practice assignment 1

For this assignment you will need to have an e-mail already sent to you. Ask your supervisor or tutor to prepare it for you. You will also need to ask for an e-mail address to send any e-mails to.

Create the following e-mail and send it to the e-mail address of the candidate:

- Virus Warning – with the message:

  'Please will you answer the questions in the attached document and send a copy of the document to all our branch offices.

  I would like you to select a stationery style to suit the business which I would like you to ask all staff to use in their e-mail correspondence.

  Desmond.'

A word processed file called 'Virus' should be attached to this e-mail message.

This should contain the following questions:

1 What is the potential harm that a virus attack could cause?
2 What should all staff do to prevent a virus attack?
3 Why should staff take care when opening file attachments?
4 What type of files might contain a virus?
5 Would a plain e-mail contain a virus?

This assignment is broken down into 6 parts:

1 A brief scenario.
2 Task A requires candidates to open a new e-mail, save a file to an appropriate location and create a folder.
3 Task B requires candidates to open an attachment, answer questions in a file and save the file.
4 Task C requires candidates to create an e-mail group with an alias.
5 Task D requires candidates to select and use a stationery style, create a signature and compose an e-mail message with a file attachment.
6 Task E requires candidates to add an e-mail address to the blocked senders list.

You must, at all times, observe all relevant health and safety precautions.

**Time allowed:** 2 hours

## Task A

1   Access your e-mail account and download, open and view the waiting e-mail. Print out a copy and label it PRINTOUT 1.

2   Save the attached file to an appropriate place to which you have access. Take a screen print of the location where you have saved the file, print out a copy and label it SCREENPRINT1.

3   Create a folder for staff information and give it an appropriate name. Move the e-mail you have received to the new folder. Take a screen print of your folder structure and obtain a printout. Label this SCREENPRINT2.

4   Switch back to your Inbox and take a screen print. Print out a copy and label it SCREENPRINT3.

5   Open the attached file and print a copy. Label it PRINTOUT2.

## Task B

1   In the opened attached file, enter your answers to the questions asked. Save the file as **E-MAIL INFORMATION** and print out a copy. Label it PRINTOUT3.

## Task C

1   Create an e-mail group with the alias name of **offices** made up of the following addresses:

Desmond Davies' e-mail address
North Office: desmonds_north@business.co.uk
South Office: desmonds_south@business.co.uk
East Office: desmonds_east@business.co.uk

Take a screen print and label it SCREENPRINT4.

2   Save the group into an address book. Take a screen print to show this and label it SCREENPRINT5.

## Task D

1   Create a suitable signature for yourself to add to your e-mail messages. Take a screen print of the signature you have created in the appropriate box before clicking the **Apply** button. Print out a copy and label it SCREENPRINT6.

**2** Select a stationery style suitable for use by the business.

**3** Start a new e-mail, using your chosen stationery style, containing the following message, to your group named **offices**:

'I attach an information notice about the risk of viruses from e-mail file attachments. Please will you print out a copy of the notice and display in the Staff Room.

Desmond would like us to use the stationery style **<insert the name of the style chosen>** in our e-mail correspondence, which has been used in this e-mail.'

Add your signature to the message. Print out a copy and label it PRINTOUT4.

**4** Find and retrieve the group addresses from the address book and address the e-mail. Take a screen print, print out a copy and label it SCREENPRINT7.

**5** Attach the file **E-MAIL INFORMATION** to the message. Take a screen print, print out a copy and label it SCREENPRINT8.

**6** Save the e-mail in your Drafts folder. Print out a copy of the e-mail and label it PRINTOUT5.

**7** Switch to your Drafts folder and take a screen print showing the e-mail waiting to be sent. Print out a copy and label it SCREENPRINT9.

# Task E

**1** A particular salesperson is constantly sending e-mail promotional literature to Desmond, and he would like you to add the name to the blocked senders list. The e-mail address of the salesperson is ste@fashionprinters.com. Add this e-mail address to the blocked senders list. Take a screen print of the blocked senders list. Print out a copy and label it SCREENPRINT10.

**2** Close down the e-mail software.

# Practice assignment 2

For this assignment you will need to have e-mails already sent to you. Ask your supervisor or tutor to prepare them for you. You will also need to ask for an e-mail address to send any e-mails to.

Create the following e-mails and send them to the e-mail address of the candidate:

- Training Day Manchester – with the message:

  'Please will you e-mail all the delegates for this event to inform them of the venue, and that a programme is attached. Please also ask for confirmation that they will be attending.

  David Gorresh
  Skills Training Agency'

- Programme Manchester – with the message:

  'Attached is the programme for the training day.'

A word processed file called 'Programme' should be attached to this e-mail message.

- Training Day Birmingham.
- Training Day London.
- Training Day Leeds.

These may contain any text.

This assignment is broken down into 3 parts:

1 A brief scenario.
2 Task A requires candidates to open a new e-mail, save a file to an appropriate location, create folders, add addresses to the address book and create an e-mail group with an alias, and draft a new e-mail, attaching a file.
3 Task B requires candidates to edit e-mail addresses in an address book, delete e-mails and folders, reply to an e-mail and create a signature.

You must, at all times, observe all relevant health and safety precautions.

**Time allowed:** 2 hours

---

**Scenario**
You are the PA to David Gorresh, the Managing Director of the Skills Training Agency. Your job is to arrange the venues for the training sessions run by the firm and to ensure that all the delegates have the correct information about time, place and the programme for the day. A series of events has been arranged over the forthcoming month and David has asked you to inform delegates about the final details of these events.

# Task A

1 Access your e-mail account and download any mail. Select the message titled **Training Day Manchester** and print out a copy. Label your printout PRINTOUT 1.

2 Save the file **Programme** to an appropriate place to which you have access. Take a screen print of the location where you have saved the file, print out a copy and label it SCREENPRINT1.

3 Create folders in your Inbox for Manchester, Birmingham, London and Leeds. Move the e-mails you have received to their appropriate folder. Take a screen print of your folder structure and obtain a print out. Label this SCREENPRINT2.

4 Add the following addresses to your address book:

Val Davies val@hotmail.com,
Joe Peters Joe@josephp.freeserve.co.uk,
Dee Smith Dee.smith@virgin.net,
Anna Lee ace@hotmail.com

Take a screen print of your address book showing the names added and produce a printout. Label it SCREENPRINT3.

5 Create a contact group for these four addresses and give it the name **Delegates**. Take a screen print of your address book showing the contact group, print out a copy and label it SCREENPRINT4.

6 Start a new message to the group with a suitable heading for the subject. Send a copy to David. Include the following message:

'The Training Day planned for next week in Manchester will be held at the Hotel Britannia. A programme for the day is attached. Please confirm that you will be able to attend.'

Attach the file **Programme** and save the message in your Drafts folder.

7 Open your Drafts folder and obtain a printout of the message. Label the printout PRINTOUT2.

# Task B

David informs you that there are some changes to the delegate list for the event and asks you to alter your contact group details accordingly.

1 The e-mail address for Joe should be: joe@josephd.freeserve.co.uk. Edit the contact details to correct the error.

2 Add the details of a new delegate, Selima Ali, whose e-mail address is s.ali@canvers.ac.uk, to your contact group. Take a screen shot of your address book after these changes and obtain a printout. Label it SCREENPRINT5.

3 Open your Drafts folder and copy the message. Start a new message to the altered group **Delegates**, and paste the message into the e-mail. Attach the file **Programme** to the new message and save it in your Drafts folder. Delete the previous message. Take a screen print of your Drafts folder, print out a copy and label it SCREENPRINT6.

4 Open your Deleted Items folder and take a screen print to show the file you have just deleted in the folder. Print out a copy and label your print SCREENPRINT7.

**5** Empty your Deleted Items folder and take a screen print to show the empty folder. Print out a copy and label it SCREENPRINT8.

**6** Open your Drafts folder and print out a copy of your message. Label it PRINTOUT3.

**7** Reply to David's original message to inform him that you have made the changes to the delegate list as requested. Print out a copy of the reply. Label it PRINTOUT4. Save your reply to David to an appropriate place to which you have access.

**8** David wishes you to add an appropriate signature to the outgoing e-mails. Create a suitable signature and add it to the message in your Drafts folder. Print out your message and label it PRINTOUT5.

**9** The event in London has been cancelled. Delete the folder you created for this event. Take a screen print of your folders list and obtain a print out. Label it SCREENPRINT9.

**10** Exit the e-mail application and close the system.

# Solutions

## Section 1 Getting Started

### Check your knowledge

**1**

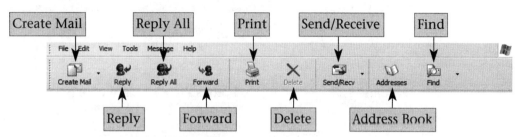

**2** See **Web-based e-mail**, page 20.

**3** See **Equipment for connecting to the Internet**, page 2.

**4**

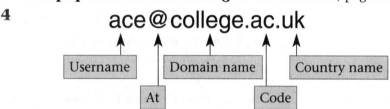

**5** **a** messages you have received
  **b** messages you have sent
  **c** message you have deleted – or nothing if the folder has been emptied.

**6** Simple Mail Transfer Protocol (SMTP) and Post Office Protocol (POP).

**7** See **How fast can you go?**, page 4.

**8** Unread messages are emboldened.

**9** See **Internet Service Providers**, page 5.

**10** Your own details.

## Section 2 Sending e-mails

### Check your knowledge

**1** Bcc (Blind Carbon Copy).

**2** Examples could include: word processed documents, images, sound files, video files, computer programs.

**3** It's taken as shouting, according to Netiquette.

**4** Cost saving, thinking time, saved as draft to complete later.

**5** Your own information.

**6** Select the attachment and delete it.

**7**

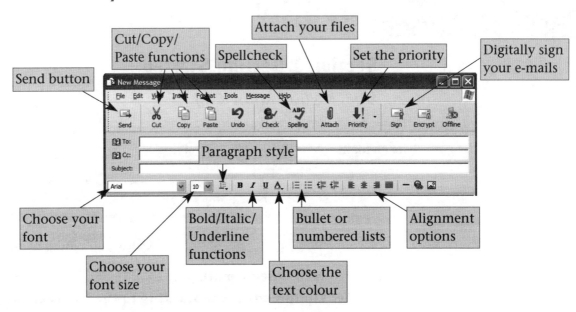

8  To maintain the privacy of a message.

9  Could include: using information already produced without having to re-type, can add to text from a document by entering it in the message box.

10  See **Finding e-mail addresses**, page 45.

## Section 3 Receiving e-mails

### *Check your knowledge*

1  See **Choosing your view**, page 49.

2  A **New Message** icon appears on the status bar.

3  See **Viruses and attachments**, page 52.

4  It is shown by a paper clip icon.

5  To tidy the Inbox.

6  Forwarding is sending the e-mail on to someone else. Replying is sending a message back to the sender.

7  See **Viewing message details**, page 61.

8  Always use a virus checker utility.

9  See **Blocking messages**, page 65.

10  See **Using automated reply methods**, page 67.

# Section 5 Using an address book

## *Check your knowledge*

**1** To enter information about your contacts.

**2**

Create new entries

View contact's details

Find addresses

Print out details

Send an e-mail to a selected contact

| New | Properties | Delete | Find People | Print | Action |

Type name or select from list:

Deletes a contact

The contact's e-mail address

**3** You will only need to enter the group name into the **To:** box instead of all the e-mail addresses individually. You won't leave anyone out of the correspondence.

**4** See **Using an address book**, page 93.

# Glossary

| | |
|---|---|
| **Attachment** | A file which is sent along with an e-mail message. |
| **Browser** | The program that allows you to view web pages on the Internet. |
| **Domain** | Part of the name for an Internet computer that tells other computers where it is and the type of organisation that owns it. |
| **Download** | Obtaining a file from a web site usually by clicking on a word or icon on the page. |
| **E-mail** | Electronic mail. A way of sending messages from one computer to another across a network. |
| **Encryption** | Files that have been coded that can't be read without a special key. |
| **Hyperlink** | Used to jump from one web page to another. Hyperlinks can be images or underlined text. |
| **Inbox** | The folder where incoming messages are placed. |
| **Internet** | The network of interconnected computers that communicate using special protocols. |
| **IP** | Internet Protocol. The system used to specify how data is transferred over the Internet. |
| **IP Address** | The unique number which identifies each computer on the Internet. |
| **ISDN** | Integrated Services Digital Network. A high-speed telephone connection which can transfer data over the Internet very quickly. |
| **ISP** | Internet Service Provider. Companies which provide a gateway to the Internet. |
| **Mailbox** | The place where e-mail is kept on an ISP server. |
| **MIME** | Multipurpose Internet Mail Extension. The system used to include non-text information, such as attached files, in an e-mail message. |
| **Netiquette** | Informal rules about the way to behave on the Internet. |
| **Network** | Computers linked together to share information and services. |
| **Offline** | Not connected to the Internet. |
| **Online** | Connected to the Internet. |
| **Online Services** | Company that provides access to its own network as well as to the Internet. |
| **Outbox** | The folder where outgoing messages are placed. |
| **POP 3** | Post Office Protocol – the protocol used to receive messages. |

| | |
|---|---|
| **Protocol** | A set of rules used by computers to communicate with each other. |
| **SMTP** | Simple Mail Transfer Protocol – the protocol used to send messages. |
| **Snail mail** | Mail delivered by the normal postal system. |
| **URL** | Universal Resource Locator. The address given to all the different resources on the Internet. |
| **Virus** | A destructive program hidden in other files and programs that can damage files on your hard drive. |
| **Web page** | A document written in HTML and linked to other documents by hyperlinks. Shown as a single screen in your browser. |